What People Are Sayir

In the rapid pace of modern culture it's easy to understand why some lag behind in their endeavor to find the best road to propel them forward. Many years ago one of my coaches told me, "If you don't gain ground, for goodness sake, don't loose ground." In other words, hold on to your plan or dream and don't allow circumstances to circumvent your goals.

Whether in middle school or middle age, Steve leads us to a valuable resource called history. He marks the course of others who discovered that a dream without a plan is an idea without legs. Steve shares his path that led him from the rank of Ensign to United States Navy Lt. Commander and from social awkwardness to Alpha Nurd.

Attaining goals is never easy. Success doesn't come cheap. Don't just read this book; use it as a tool to open the door to your greatness—to be a world changer!

— Joe Jackson
NFL, Minnesota Vikings and New York Jets defensive end

This is an incredible book! I was captivated and motivated by every page. I believe there is a nurd within all of us. Embrace it and let it work for you. Thank you, Commander Steve Rampton.

— Guy Eastman
Retired US Naval Commander, USNA 1968

I love how Steve Rampton unfolds periods of nurd history. Many shakers and movers in life have been misunderstood and misrepresented. I was enlightened and encouraged by this read!

— Dr. G. Craig Lauterbach
Founder and President, LifeWord Publishing

Do you want to know why so many people are unhappy with their lives and their work? They just settle for the easy road. In *Alpha*

Nurd, Steve Rampton takes us into the lives of many successful people, from Socrates to Steve Jobs, to share inspiring insights into fulfillment in life. The Japanese people have a concept of work that is sort of like paradise or nirvana; it brings together these ideas that you can use as you find your special life path. Do:

- What do you like to do the most
- What you are good at doing
- What can give you good income
- What benefits society

Alpha Nurd will lead you on that pathway.

— Dr. David E. Schroeder
Chancellor, Pillar College

ALPHA

TREND SETTER

WORLD CHANGER

NURD

STEVE RAMPTON

Foreword by LEE ROUSON

LWP
LIFEWORD PUBLISHING

Alpha Nurd: The Historical Revolution of Nerds/Nurds

© 2022 by Steven Rampton. All rights reserved.

LifeWord Publishing
Post Office Box 201
Pipersville, PA 18947 USA

Unless otherwise noted, all scripture quotations are taken from the King James Version, which is in public domain.

Library of Congress Preassigned Control Number: 2022901335

ISBN: 978-1-7363911-4-3 (Print)

         978-1-7363911-5-0 (E-book)

Printed in the United States of America

Ideas from a baby boomer combat vet working on his bucket list.

For all the misunderstood geeks and techies out there. Each of us has at least one special skill. My son says all things seen and unseen are ART—so find and exercise your inner artist.

What is purposed for evil

God turns for good.

Dedication

To my grandfathers: Herman Kehl, a pioneer in seed development to enhance his flower business in Louisville, Ohio; and Frank Rampton who, to make ends meet in the Great Depression, set up a still in his basement and developed equipment to create a vacuum in his old oak barrels to artificially age and sell his moonshine. He often carried President Truman to Kansas City on his Rock Island train. As conductor, Grandpa Rampton thought he was the train boss, even if the President was on board.

To my loving grandmothers Leila Kehl and Effie Rampton, who put up with and supported my grandfathers.

To my mother, Esther Kehl Rampton, the oldest girl of eight children, for being a guiding light and a culinary inspiration. She often tried new ingredients and herbs in her cooking to improve taste and nutrition.

To my father, Dr. Francis Robert Rampton, whom my sister Nancy McAlister described on his headstone as "the maker of smiles." He grew up dirt poor in Iowa, bought his own clothes from age 12 onward, and worked his way through dental and orthodontic schools to become the first orthodontist in Jacksonville, Florida. He was a true artist with his hands and wires to create smiles in 25,000 patients. Much love to my sister Linda Shore and brother Frank Rampton too.

To my wife, nicknamed Noah, the oldest daughter of three from Michigan, who is fearless in her life journey and in her spirit. She is bold and beautiful.

To our "most excellent" children Steve, Susanna, and Shannon. We lost four to miscarriage and raised three beautiful children. They are an artist, a nurse, and a teacher/coach. The responsibility of raising them made many decisions easy because they were my highest priority while they grew up.

To the United States Navy for my baptism of fire in Vietnam. Where else could you personally supervise 56 men and a nuclear weapon at age 24? I grew up very quickly—I had no choice. Many lives depended on it.

To my football friends J.C. Gouse and Glenn Klein who have been waiting three years to know "the word."

Contents

Foreword

From the moment I made the final cut for the 1972 O'Henry Lions Pop Warner football team in Greensboro, North Carolina, as the only African American to make the team, I did not fit in. I remember my coach saying, "We have one more person to make the team, Cecil Lee Rouson III." As I walked over to my new teammates, who were all white kids, away from all of my friends, who were all black kids, it was the first time in my life when I felt like I didn't fit in.

The saga continued in high school where I struggled to fit in even though I lettered in three sports and served as student body president my last year.

When I left Greensboro to attend the University of Colorado as a scholarshiped student athlete, again I was acutely conscious of not fitting in. Many of my peers let me know that they thought that even though I was famous, I wasn't going to make it in college because "the white man was going to keep me down."

Most of my teammates were from big cities like LA, Miami, New York, Chicago, Houston, and Detroit. I was seen as a country boy from North Carolina. My core belief was that my future was bright and that I was going to make it to the NFL. As always, it was an uphill battle because after I arrived, Colorado was put on NCAA probation for something that happened thirteen years prior to any current coach or athlete being there.

The good news is that I was drafted into the NFL by the New York Giants football club in 1985. I was surrounded by some of the best college football players in the United States. Most were well known. Me, not so much. Whenever my name came up, the response was "Lee who"? Once again, I didn't fit in. Well, I made the team and helped win two Super Bowl championships.

In a way, not fitting in has been the best challenge/motivator in my life.

I thank my friend Steve Rampton for writing this insightful book. Whoever feels or sees themselves as not fitting in, it's okay. Think of yourself as being unique and keep moving forward toward your goals.

—Lee Rouson

Two-time NFL Super Bowl champ with the New York Giants, professional motivational speaker, and principal executive of Move Your Chains, LLC

Preface

The highest calling is to perform a creative act. For an architect, it's a new structure. For a poet, new verses. For an artist, an amazing new work. For a spiritual man, a healing. For the Supreme it is fulfilling his creative essence—his being, his Nature.

I am writing this book for you as an individual because ultimately that is what we are judged as. I also recognize that this might be used as a resource for mentors and teachers, so I have included historical facts and perspectives.

The highest calling is to perform a creative act.

Most important for me, it is to inspire you to analyze, plan, and create your own life, your best life—your own legacy. After all, as Socrates said, "The unexamined life is not worth living."

Introduction

There's no such thing as coincidence.

There's a reason for everything in your life.

There's a reason you are reading this introduction to my book about world changers.

Your life is shaped by many influences and influencers. Circumstances like where you were born; who you were born to as parents, guardians, and grandparents; who you hang out with as friends, classmates, coaches, teachers, and coworkers. They all can be positive, negative, or neutral. Who knows, you might even be influenced by a mentor, like me.

Your life is shaped by many influences and influencers.

I have met two world changers. The first was Alan B. Shepard, Jr., the first American in space. The second was Steve Jobs, one of three founders of Apple. It is rare meeting a true world changer, but I am confident that neither was a coincidence.

Rear Admiral Shepard was an unexpected meeting in 1961 along with my uncle Colonel Raymond Kehl, an Air Force pilot. Steve Jobs and I were on board the same cross-country airline flight in the 1980s. The conversation focused on his new company and his new Macintosh personal computer. It was both inspiring and intimidating. In Chapter Six, I describe how he asked me lots of questions; his perspective was he saw the light at the end of his tunnel and was very focused on getting there. That's what I want for you. Be focused. There are a lot of distractions out there.

My personal picture of life is me standing firm while a tornado of people and events whirls around me. My main job is to stand, but I have to deal with the daily stuff floating by. I have to stay centered on what I must do to work out my life plan. Inspirational meetings like the above intensify the fire to make the plan work.

This book is about inspiring *your* life and coming up with *your* plan. Doing what I call "the dailies" to work it out. I describe dozens of others (both male and female) who have completed their quests. Now it's *your* turn to be a world changer.

No matter their age, one person can make a difference!

Chapter One: Beginnings

T iming is everything. Since graduating in 1966 from The Bolles School, a prep school in Jacksonville, Florida, I have been running a marathon. I did my undergrad at Vanderbilt University, then went straight into the US Navy. I served on active duty for three years and reserves for three years, attaining the rank of lieutenant commander and going to Vietnam, where I did not enjoy getting shot at frequently. After that I went to graduate school at Tulane University, got married, endured four miscarriages with my lovely wife, and then raised three beautiful children while working. The years have flown by, but I have always carried the acorn of this book in my heart. Hopefully you are wondering where my word "nurd" came from. Well, it is time to let my acorn grow into a tree.

I want to acknowledge something up front: I am not the only person who came up with the word "nerd/nurd." I am probably the first to apply it to humans, however. There is a concept used in scientific discovery, which is to consider what was "in the wind" at a specific time—meaning that often several people will come with the same discovery at roughly the same time. Scientific examples of multiple independent discoveries of similar subject matter include the concept of calculus from Sir Isaac Newton and Gottfried Wilhelm Leibniz in the 17th century; the discovery of oxygen from

Carl Wilhelm Schede, Joseph Priestly, and Antoine Lavoisier in the 18th century; the theory of evolution by Charles Darwin and Alfred Russel Wallace; and the lightning rod from Benjamin Franklin and Prokop Diviš.

I'll leave it to you, the reader, as to whether the concept of nerd/nurd falls into that category of discovery.

First of all, "nurd" is not a misspelling of "nerd." It *is* a worldwide phenomenon. For example, you have probably heard of Nerds™ candy. There are TV shows like *King of Nerds* and movies such as *Revenge of the Nerds*, *The Nerd*, and *Angry Video Game Nerd—The Movie*. There is also a music group called N*E*R*D*, whose most famous member is Pharrel Williams.

"Nurd" is not a misspelling of "nerd." It *is* a worldwide phenomenon.

If you look up *nerd* on Wikipedia, it says it refers to an intelligent but single-minded person obsessed with a nonsocial hobby or pursuit. Nerds are generally considered to be awkward, shy, and/or unattractive by most.[1] There is also an entry for NuRD, a complex in molecular biology "with both ATP-dependent chromatin remodeling and histone deacetylase activities."[2] I don't think that one is what we're looking for. Maybe from the small village of Nur, the capital of Nur county in Iran? No.

In the World English Dictionary they list nerd *or* nurd: "A boring or unpopular person, especially one obsessed with something specified: a computer nerd or 2. A stupid and feeble person."[3]

Stupid and feeble? No way.

Chapter One: Beginnings

I want to lay a foundation for my version of the word *nurd* and let you draw your own conclusions. In 2019, I watched the movie *The Professor and the Madman*. In the movie, William Minor, a Civil War physician, becomes an avid researcher for James Murray, a largely self-educated man from Scotland, who is tasked with writing the original Oxford Dictionary. Both men worked hard to go back as far as they could to each word's beginning in the English language. This movie confirmed to me that the etymology of a word *is* important and renewed my motivation to write *Alpha Nurd*.

My thoughts on what it means to be a nurd really began in high school and college. I think of myself as Tess from *Working Girl*. Have you seen that film? It is a 1988 romantic comedy involving a Staten Island "working girl" secretary, Tess, working M&A (mergers and acquisitions) who took advantage of a situation to push her idea and improve her career. When her boss tried to take credit for the brilliant idea, the big boss tried to get to the bottom of the controversy, asking both women where the idea or "spark" came from. Her boss had no clue because it was not hers. Tess spoke up and had every detail. She was the true author. That's me—I have every detail.

My word *nurd*, ironically, came from another movie—*Good Neighbor Sam*. It is a 1964 comedy starring Jack Lemmon and one of my favorites, Edward G. Robinson. Jack plays an ad executive named Sam Bissell. One of his most important clients is Simon Nurdlinger (Edward G. Robinson), CEO of Nurdlinger Dairies. Now you have a hint. Nurdlinger is thinking of taking his dairy advertising business elsewhere because he suspects abnormal behavior at the ad agency and he only likes super straight arrows in life—basic family values and no funny business.

I took the rather odd-sounding family name and made the word *nurdlinger* into a noun or adjective. So in 1964 and onward I used it to characterize other people. Funny. Cheesy. Dorky. Super smart. I started using the phrase "don't be such a nurdlinger," meaning super straight and kind of boring. After a while I shortened it to "don't be such a nurd," or just calling someone a nurd. It became part of my vocabulary for the rest of my life—living in Florida, Tennessee, in the US Navy all over the world, Louisiana, Wyoming, and New Jersey. There is no telling how many thousands of people I have come into contact with and shared the term with since then.

As of 2019, Wikipedia notes the origin of the word *nerd* is obviously before this book. That's okay with me. I have read the account of the Dr. Seuss book *If I Ran the Zoo*, where the narrator says he would collect "a Nerkle, a Nerd, and a Seersucker too"[4]—cool animal creatures in his world but no relevance to people. Wikipedia does note that the alternative spelling of "nurd" appeared in the mid '60s or early '70s. That's about right, since I started using it after the movie came out in 1964. I also want to tip my hat to science fiction author Philip K. Dick, who used the spelling of "nurd" in 1973.

In 1964 and onward I used the word *nurdlinger* to characterize other people. Funny. Cheesy. Dorky. Super smart.

But remember, I started using the word *nurd* in the '60s. My hope is that the Online Etymology Dictionary will pick up my unique derivation. I think of it as a compliment that it was in use at Rensselaer Polytechnic Institute (RPI) and then at MIT about 1971, where it was used because it sounds like the word *drunk* spelled backward. Also special thanks to Henry Winkler and Ron Howard for making it popular in the '70s with their show *Happy Days*.

The words *nerd* and *nerdlinger* (or for me, *nurd*) are still being used today. You can find the word *nerdlinger* in *The Simpsons* episode "Homer Goes to College." It's also used to describe a fan of the show *Futurama*. You can find it in the names of websites such as *Nerdist*, Nerdtests.com, and Nerdwallet.com (for more examples see Appendix A).

I know I'm going to catch some heat and disbelief, but hopefully being able to track the derivation of *nurd* to a specific time and place will improve my credibility. I suggest you watch *Good Neighbor Sam*. I studied electrical engineering at Vanderbilt until Uncle Sam called; I never read Dr. Seuss or anything from Philip K. Dick, although he sounds interesting. The DNA of my word *nurd* is clean. I really can't say the same for the others except Dr. Seuss. My motives were to cope with or make fun of other students with a private joke. To me, that in itself sounds "nurdy." I was one of the smart ones in high school (top three), so I was not accustomed to *not* being one of the smartest in the room. At Vanderbilt everyone was smart so I had to learn to cope. I felt like I didn't fit in this new environment. Academics was a challenge, and socially I was an outcast. *Nurd* was a play on words and a small element in dealing with life. Even now I call that coping with my struggles or my "dailies."

Another place I might get heat is, "Where have you been for 50 years?" Just saying "busy" is not enough. Life has a way of devouring your time on a daily basis and now I'm facing some health challenges. College. Military. Career. Wife. Children. I'm writing this now to let the world know that I had a part to play in this word's origin. I want my children and, to date, grandson to know that one person *can* make a difference in this world. Think about it. If you ask ten Americans what a *nurd* is, I bet all ten will have an idea. Even if you go to Africa, Asia, and the Far East people will say they've heard the word. Of course the TV shows, movies, and candy name help. Its connotations are not always positive. Think of it this way:

the president's home here in America was berated at first as Mr. Jefferson's white house mess. Now everyone knows it as *The* White House. For another example of how my mind works see Appendix B. Things change.

Chapter Two: Influencers

In the movie *Contact*, researchers were looking for alien life and were able to pull television audio and video from space. When they did, they heard the voice of Adolph Hitler welcoming the Olympic athletes to the Berlin Games. Theoretically this is possible. Basic concept: energy is forever. Once it's out there, you can't take it back.

What happens when you speak? Your lungs and voice box work together to vibrate your vocal chords creating energy to make a sound. And that sound energy goes on forever. It's one thing to have an idea and another to put legs under it—that is, to verbalize it. Every word you say does not just go out there and fizzle away to nothing like Alka Seltzer. The words are out there—forever, so be careful what you say.

Reflect back on your life. Who or what has been a big influence? Let's start with your family—your mother, father, grandmother, or aunt? First, you were a creation from your mother and father. Whether an "oops" or "in vitro," you were created from the DNA of two people. Your fingerprints are like no other on the face of the Earth. Some of my friends also use the snowflake analogy—even in a snowstorm that leaves trillions of snowflakes in the form of a foot of snow, no two are alike. That fact alone means you are pretty amazing.

And how did you get to where you are today? By yourself? No. You had parents or guardians to assist and teachers to encourage. In my mind, I see King Leonidas of the Spartans from the movie *300*. As a 12-year-old boy, he was out in the snow all by himself with shabby clothes and his wooden spear. A huge black wolf with fire in his eyes was stalking him, hungry to make a meal of the young king. Spartans are tough on their young boys. If you are alive, then you have learned much, especially to survive. Leonidas had to draw upon all his training. He kept calm and lured the huge beast into a chasm where he could fit, but the bigger animal could not. When the wolf charged to make the kill, he was wedged between the large rocks, presenting an easy target for the young king to kill him with his spear. Leonidas learned and survived. I want you to be the same. It's good to step back and recognize people and events that helped get you to where you are today.

> # It's good to step back and recognize people and events that helped get you to where you are today.

Please consider the story of a son and daughter on the West Coast, born into a wealthy family. Their parents were killed in a car crash when they were teenagers and they inherited all the money. Their standard of living was high, and the son continued in his free-spending ways—drugs, sex, and rock and roll. The daughter had fun and enjoyed her life but learned to cut down on the lifestyle and put away some money where she could not touch it. Time went by. Money was slipping away. The son realized that he could not continue his lifestyle but had no plans or experience with an alternative lifestyle. When the money was almost gone the son decided he could not cope in this world without money, so he killed himself. It's a sad story. His parents weren't around to support or consult. No peer wanted to give up the party atmosphere so they went along as long as the money lasted. Money gone? Oh well. Find another friend.

So what's your situation? On your own? Have a few friends? Have a supportive family? There are a few basic rules of life we can talk about that I guarantee will help.

Chapter Three: Life Lessons

Take the Blue Pill or the Red Pill?

In the 1999 film *The Matrix,* the character Neo is asked by Morpheus to take one of two pills. The red pill will take him to the harsh reality of life and the blue pill will allow him to stay in the comfortable illusion of a false reality. Looking at the multibillion-dollar video game industry, I wonder how many millions have chosen the blue pill. I find this sad because you only get one shot at this thing called "life," and it would be a shame to waste it.

> # You only get one shot at this thing called "life," and it would be a shame to waste it.

I grew up middle class in Florida. My dad was an orthodontist, and my mother was a stay-at-home mom with a nursing degree, which she used after her kids grew up. When I was 16 my parents divorced, and a year later I was on my own at college. I finished at The Bolles School and headed to Vanderbilt University, known as the "Harvard of the South," as an engineer and Navy ROTC student. I have not lived at home since I was 18. I have traveled about a million miles in ships, 2 million in airplanes, and 1.5 million in cars. I had to make it work because I did not have a backup plan. So I guess you could say I swallowed the red pill.

How did I do it? On reflection I followed some basic rules:

1. **You are the captain of your ship.** You control your thought life. Make sure the thoughts are positive and constructive. When you have an idea, take control of it and run with it. Try to come up with a life plan and work that plan. Change it every day if you need to, but have a plan. It can be helpful to keep a notebook or diary to keep track of your plan and your course corrections.

2. **Don't be afraid to start at the bottom because if you are any good you won't be there long.** After all, if you demonstrate that you do a good job and can be trusted with little, then it is more likely someone is going to give you bigger, greater things and responsibilities.

3. **Quality is better than quantity**. It is better to do some good work than it is to do a lot of crappy work. Guard your reputation and your integrity.

4. **Don't be afraid to fail.** Colonel Sanders had 11 jobs by 1955, and at 65 years old all he had was Social Security and his chicken recipes. He worked hard and hit it big with Kentucky Fried Chicken. Thomas Edison tried hundreds of filaments for his incandescent light bulb before he found the magic wire (carbonized bamboo filament) that met his specifications—it lasted more than a few seconds and was practical for commercial applications.

5. **Common sense goes further than raw intelligence.** One example of this is the true story of a high school senior who was headed to be valedictorian and a medical doctor. He had a flat tire on a date. For whatever reason, he could not change the tire. Luckily a state trooper came by and helped him put on the spare. The next morning his father heard the story and promptly had his son out in the driveway changing every tire on the car, making sure he knew how to do it. The point is raw intelligence is not enough. You need a dose of common sense to go with it.

One of my past bosses asked me to help him hire a new plant engineer. I was to bring him a list of five prequalified men or women. They had to get past me to get to him. His only instruction to me from his 30 years of experience was *no* straight-A students. He had not had good luck with them. He said he wanted someone with a lot of common sense, so grades were second priority (Bs were OK) and common sense first.

6. **Work for yourself, not others—especially in your spare time.** One good friend of mine rarely watches TV. The reason? One of his past bosses heard him talk about all the TV shows he used to watch. His comment to my friend was, "Do you realize that you are making someone else rich by watching their shows?" He was right—people spend and make millions on advertisements and ratings. So now he reads skill-enhancing books and is trying to improve his resume— not enhance someone else's.

7. I'm going to change a popular phrase a little: **Keep your family close and your friends closer.** Both will encourage. Get friends you can hang out with on a daily basis and can build your social and work network with—but remember bad company corrupts eventually, so don't forget to cull out the sheep, goats, and wolves. Some friends can be wolves.

My job as a mentor is not to fill in all the blanks in your life but to point you in the most productive direction. These steps worked for me.

Chapter Four: Social Strata

L et's get back to the concept of *nurd*.

I see the world in terms of social stratification. Other terms are the haves and have-nots, lords or ladies and commoners, or classes and castes. *My* social worldview is sheep, wolves, and nurds.

The vast majority of people in the world are social sheep. They want to survive, so they look for the easiest way. They find a niche that provides for most of their needs and follow that path like a lowly sheep. Unfortunately, it does not allow for much opportunity because as a sheep you are probably not making great money; more often than not, bosses will not pay you what you are worth—that way the company makes money instead of you. You also likely do not have much free time. That is one of the reasons people are obsessed with making the most of weekends. That time is truly theirs.

The wolves are out there waiting to see whom they can pounce on and devour. Remember my reference to King Leonidas of the Spartans? A big hungry wolf was stalking him. It's the same in society. Some people view themselves as bigger, stronger, or smarter.

They look for easy targets to take advantage of or maneuver. Unfortunately, these targets are the sheep I referenced before. The worst wolves are in politics and religion.

Then there are the nurds. These are past sheep or wolves who somehow break through the economic or mental barriers to be creative. Many have what my wife is blessed with, and that is tunnel vision—they can block the whole world out and concentrate on one thing at a time and get the most from it. In her case it's dealing with numbers. She is amazing, but don't ask her a question when she is "in the zone." You will either get a grunt or no answer at all. The nurds are the people who ask "why not?" when the sheep ask "why?" Why not change? Why not try another solution? Why not write a book?

Most people are caught up doing what I call "mini-max." People want to get maximum results in their lives from minimum effort. I guess the ultimate example of this is the lottery—you put in $1.00 and hope to reap millions.

> # Most people are caught up doing what I call "mini-max." People want to get maximum results in their lives from minimum effort.

Let's reflect back on your schooling. You ask around to find out what courses or instructors can get you the best grade for the minimum amount of work—kind of like a "no show" job. You never have to go in and do anything, but you get a paycheck anyway. I don't personally know anyone like this, but it certainly happens in government and at high levels in corporations such as certain committees of the Board of Directors.

So how does mini-max tie together with the sheep, the wolves, and the nurds? Well the sheep are mini-maxers because they are looking to survive with the least amount of effort. The little mouse scurries around until he finds food sources and then he gets lazy, going back to the same ones till they are gone. These are like the friends of the young heir from my previous illustration, who partied with him till the money was gone and then he died. The wolves are mini-maxers because they find a food source like a herd of elk and follow that herd as long as they can, picking off one elk per week to feed their families.

The nurds are the exception. Yes, they also need to eat, but they are looking for a better way to survive. They are the Polynesian sailor who is looking for a new island to inhabit where he does not have to compete with all the other natives for females and food. They are the innovators like John D. Rockefeller who discovered a better and cheaper way to make kerosene to light homes and factories. Because of his innovation, society no longer has to depend on killing whales to get whale oil. His innovative drive as a nurd brought huge environmental and social positive impact. You can be the same, but you need to fine tune *your* choices and path.

Chapter Five: Influential Americans

Innovators through History

L et's put all this into perspective. I've been talking the human side. Now let's look at the physical and technical side. Starting from ancient times, what do you think are the most important technical and cultural advancements of all time? From the discovery of fire to the invention of the Internet, where did these marvelous inventions or technical leaps come from? Yes, some were accidents—like the adhesive for the Post-it® Note—but most were the culmination of many small steps and failures of people (nurds) who kept following their path or their dream. Those who succeeded gained power and influence (with the notable exception of Nikola Tesla). See Appendix C for a full listing of major steps.

Society generally rewards "the winner." I guess I don't mind that too much because it gets back to providing goods and services that people want/demand. Unfortunately the rewards (money) are sometimes lop sided. I have a secret desire that there could be million dollar teachers, not just million dollar athletes.

Influential Americans

Remember, the subtitle of this book is that one person can make a difference. Let's take a look at a listing of the most influential people in the history of the United States. I hope teachers will use the list not only to point out how nurds changed the world, but as a mini history lesson of how the United States labor force moved so quickly from farms to factories.

In 2006, *The Atlantic* published an issue titled "The 100 Most Influential Americans of All Time," compiled from the input of historians, editors, and readers. Their top ten were:

1. Abraham Lincoln
2. George Washington
3. Thomas Jefferson
4. Franklin Roosevelt
5. Alexander Hamilton
6. Benjamin Franklin
7. John Marshall
8. Martin Luther King, Jr.
9. Thomas Edison
10. Woodrow Wilson

Others of note are: John D. Rockefeller (11), Henry Ford (14), Andrew Carnegie (20), Orville and Wilbur Wright (23), Alexander Graham Bell (24), Albert Einstein (32), and J.P. Morgan (37).[5]

Hopefully you recognize most or all of the people on the list. I would argue that the people on this list are not sheep or wolves—they are nurds. You might accuse me of circular reasoning because I only allowed for three classifications, but think about it. What kind of people are out there? There are those who *do* and those who *don't*.

There *are* those who are unable or disabled through no fault of their own. But that does not mean they cannot be world changers. Do you know who Stephen Hawking was? He was a theoretical physicist and cosmologist at Cambridge University—an eccentric and a loner. But some considered him the smartest guy on the planet. Oh, by the way—he had motor neuron disease and could not walk or talk, except by the use of a special computer. He was disabled, but he did not let that stop him. Your limitations don't have to stop you from being a nurd!

OK, just in case you don't trust my criteria, let's talk about some of these men. For you ladies out there, your list will come a little later because I have a lot to say about the advantages of being female.

So what did these guys do that was so great?

Abraham Lincoln

Abraham Lincoln started his life in a one-room log cabin in Kentucky and became President of the United States. He held the Union together and paved the way for the emancipation of slaves in the South. His actions helped establish the national value that it was not acceptable to have another human being serving you without compensation or opportunity to leave. Being enslaved is even worse than being a sheep; they at least have some fundamental choices, but a slave has none.

George Washington

George Washington took the reins of a loose association of states, strengthened the federal government into a true nation, and handed the reins back. He actually paid his own way during the Revolutionary War—no one sent him a paycheck—and used his expense account to help pay for those around him. After his presidency, he did not stick around Washington for as long as possible to feather his own bed or come back as a consultant or industry rep. He actually gave the reins of power back once his term was over instead of becoming a new emperor or king. This decision established the tradition of peaceful transfer of power in the United States that has continued ever since.

Thomas Jefferson

Thomas Jefferson used his wit, oratory, and writing skills to sew together the right words to form landmark documents, such as the Declaration of Independence, that can be seen in the Library of Congress or Constitution Hall in Philadelphia. He was a complex man; while he was wealthy and a slave owner, he tried three times to pass emancipation legislation and decried slavery as a moral wrong. He or other males in his family probably fathered all of the children of Sally Hemmings, one of his slaves.

Franklin Roosevelt

Along with his amazing wife Eleanor, Franklin Roosevelt planted many trees (environmentalists)—and also ideas about safety, security, and helping those who cannot help themselves. Like Abraham Lincoln, he held together the Union—this time during a world war. He was confined to a wheelchair, but with the help of the press he kept his chin up and the confidence of the American people.

Alexander Hamilton

Alexander Hamilton had a cool house called Hamilton Grange in what is now Harlem. He used the house to entertain dignitaries to get them to help him turn our agrarian economy into industry. He was an avid supporter of the Constitution, and as the first Treasury Secretary he built a strong financial foundation for our young country. He was also the mastermind behind Paterson Great Falls in

New Jersey—the first industrial park with its own power source—water. Also, how cool is it to have a hit Broadway show with your name on it?

Ben Franklin

Ben Franklin was the American Rudolph Valentino of his day. He was a great schmoozer and negotiator. He was part actor and part lover. Early Pennsylvanian currency was actually printed by him. His work helped establish the foundation of a value system for American money. In Europe he was widely known as a ladies' man. Doesn't really come off if you look at a portrait. Well, he was smart, good with words, and played three musical instruments. Very cool guy. His resume, like Jefferson's, makes me dizzy because they were so good at many things.

John Marshall

John Marshall helped solidify the Supreme Court as a strong third branch of government. It is the final stop in the judiciary chain. It interprets law based on the Constitution that the founding fathers wrote and ratified. The founding fathers recognized that there indeed are sheep and wolves and laid a foundation to protect all. Sometimes the nurds have a cooler head and act as the referee in our system of government. Basically, creativity is great in science but often not a good idea in trying to take advantage of another person. Twisting the law to suit you is not a good idea, and the justice system, strengthened under John Marshall, helped to mitigate those kinds of abuses.

Martin Luther King

Dr. Martin Luther King, Jr. was definitely not a sheep. His life and ministry was about people, equality, and purpose. This definitely is nurdy thinking outside the normal societal box.

Thomas Edison

Thomas Edison is the first geek on the list. He is widely known as the Wizard of Menlo Park. His curiosity (remember: "why not?") led him to inventions that changed the whole world. Just think of what percentage of our modern life depends on lights and electrical power—like this computer that I am typing on (or using speech-to-text on). He invented the first commercially viable incandescent light, electrical distribution systems, the stock ticker, motion picture machines, and many other useful products. I recently learned the technology of his electric pen was the start of the modern tattoo machines.

Woodrow Wilson

Woodrow Wilson was President from 1913 to 1921 and leader of the progressive movement. He helped hold the world together during World War I. He sponsored the League of Nations (the predecessor of the United Nations), for which he won the 1919 Nobel Peace Prize. His progressive party ushered in the Federal Reserve Act, the FTC, women's right to vote, and an income tax.

John D. Rockefeller

John D. Rockefeller was raised mainly by his frugal mother in New York and Ohio. He was well behaved and studious. That served him well in the oil refinery business where his nurdy ideas were able to improve the refining process, cut costs, and sign a great transportation deal with Cornelius Vanderbilt for use of his railroads. He experimented with using kerosene in place of whale oil (a big deal for whales) and grew that business to the nationwide Standard Oil Company. He, Vanderbilt, Carnegie, and J.P. Morgan were the big four in industrializing the United States, creating millions of jobs, and perfecting the fine art of philanthropy.

Henry Ford

Henry Ford was all about the assembly line and cars, cars, and more cars. I could include him in the above four names as being a part of the industrializing of America. His nurdy ideas helped perfect the assembly line and improved the technology of machines. He was a frequent visitor at Edison's workshop in New Jersey, always looking for new and better ideas.

Andrew Carnegie

Andrew Carnegie was to the steel industry as Rockefeller was to petroleum refining. Rockefeller built up Cleveland, Ohio. Carnegie built up Pittsburgh, Pennsylvania. He was born in Scotland to very poor parents. Once here he built himself up with sales and investments. Once he concentrated on making steel, he built up the Carnegie Steel Company in Pittsburgh. He sold it in 1901 to J.P. Morgan for $480 million ($13 billion in today's money) and formed U.S. Steel. He ended up giving away 90 percent of his fortune through philanthropy (he was big on building libraries) and setting the tone for other wealthy individuals. Definitely nurdy.

The Wright Brothers

Orville and Wilbur Wright were brothers who ran a printing business and then a bicycle repair and sales shop in Ohio. Their fascination with controlled, powered flight led to the invention of the first airplane. But for us it was much more. Other geeks saw the possibilities and airlines became one of the biggest businesses. Travel was enhanced. The world became a little smaller.

Alexander Graham Bell

Alexander Graham Bell was greatly influenced by the need to help his wife and mother, both of whom were deaf. He did much in his life with aeronautics and optical telecommunications, but we remember him for inventing the first practical telephone.

Telecommunications is huge for us. He saw a world where people could be connected in a brand new way. Like the Wright brothers with airlines, it made our world a little smaller.

Albert Einstein

Albert Einstein was as big or even bigger than the before-mentioned Stephen Hawking. He is geek number four. Einstein was born in Germany and became an American citizen in 1940. Well-known as a theoretical scientist, he won the Nobel Prize for Physics in 1921. He developed one of the two main precepts of modern physics—the general theory of relativity. The other is quantum mechanics. Yes, he developed the energy-mass equivalency equation of $E=mc^2$, but what I like about him is the new label (like nurd) we put on people, calling them Einsteins (geniuses).

J.P. Morgan

J.P. Morgan and Alexander Hamilton would have been best buds. Hamilton was all about banking and finance and so was J.P. Morgan. Both loved the art of the deal—Hamilton in starting early American finance and Morgan in arranging the merger of Edison General Electric with Thomas-Houston Electric into the current General Electric or just GE. Also, as noted with Andrew Carnegie, Morgan bought his Carnegie Steel Company and other smaller firms and formed United States Steel Corporation or just U.S. Steel. He also participated in the fine art of philanthropy like Rockefeller, Vanderbilt, and Carnegie.

These men had a huge impact on the forming of our great nation and moving the economy from an agrarian base to an industrial one. Around 1900 more than 60 percent of workers were in farming or servicing farmers. Then after Rockefeller, Carnegie, Ford, and Morgan were done, fully 50 percent of the work force was in the industrial sector. We will talk about the latest shift to technology a little later.

Where do the geeks come in? They followed the Golden Rule of History: "They that have the gold make the rules." Some call these men "robber barons" because they developed their industries but took advantage of their workers. Others called them captains of industry who grew their businesses, improved their own lives, and the lives of millions of workers. More "gold" in their pockets. Those who think ahead get ahead.

The nurds have pointed the way for technical and innovative solutions to problems.

Look at China now. Hundreds of millions of people have left their farming homes and come into the cities to improve their lives and send some money back home, thus improving the lives of their families. Some 550 million are still on the farms. We here in the United States now have 2 percent of our workers on farms and 12 percent in businesses and industry. We are fighting for our industrial lives because other countries have awakened to the fact that if they can somehow grow or move businesses from the United States to their region, their economy and people will greatly benefit. Don't blame them and don't blame the US companies for moving because they can make more "gold" overseas. It's all about economics.

In summary, the geeks have been very important for the United States. The nurds have pointed the way for technical and innovative solutions to problems. It's the "why not" syndrome. Now let's look at the world view.

Chapter Six: World Changing Males

et's shift gears a little from just American to worldwide influencers. Ranker lists the world's most influential people of all time. I like it because it's crowdsourced from people all over the world, so it is a collective opinion rather than one person's idea. To be on their list you must have a significant effect on common people and on how society works. Again the concept of sheep, wolves, and nurds comes into play. As you read this, see which of these you would put into each category. The order changes over time, but in 2018 they were:

1. Jesus Christ
2. Muhammad
3. Isaac Newton
4. Aristotle
5. Leonardo da Vinci
6. Albert Einstein
7. Galileo Galilei
8. Plato
9. Charles Darwin
10. Alexander the Great

11. Socrates
12. Nikola Tesla
13. Gautama Buddha
14. Moses
15. George Washington
16. Confucius
17. Mahatma Gandhi
18. William Shakespeare
19. Johannes Gutenberg
20. Abraham Lincoln

Others of interest to me are Henry Ford (38), the Wright brothers (40), Bill Gates (48), James Watt (60), Steve Jobs (71), Gene Roddenberry (152), and Steven Spielberg (167).

Jesus Christ

Jesus had many names. Jesus Christ. Jesus of Nazareth. Jesus, son of Joseph. In Greek He was a *tekton*, a term meaning craftsman or artisan. I find it very interesting that this has the same root as our words *technical* and *technology*. So maybe we could call Him the maker of technical things 2,000 years ago. I guess a carpenter would qualify. We know how important technology has been for the world. He is the main character in the bestselling book of all time, the Bible.

So why did Ranker put Him in as the number one influence on world history? Well, the criterion is having a significant effect on common people and/or on how society works. Martin Luther King, Jr. and Mahatma Gandhi agreed with His teaching on non-violence and used that technique in getting civil rights for their people. Moses and He agreed on the basic Ten Commandments (no, not suggestions) for living. My generation of flower children would agree with His thoughts on the importance of love. He wanted us to love the Supreme and each other and to treat each other as we want them to treat us.

His followers were mainly sheep. The poor and sick came to Him like magnets because He provided for all their needs (their mini-max man). He was not a wolf, however, like Jim Jones who, when he thought his life and ministry were over, gave hundreds of his followers "the Kool Aid," which was laced with cyanide. They all died. Jesus was a threat to the power of the Jewish hierarchy of His day, so they condemned Him and used their influence with the Roman governor to get him to condemn Jesus to death on the cross. Note, however, that He did not take His disciples or followers with Him. He went alone. His "gospel" or good news continued after He was dead and spread through the Middle East, Africa, and Europe. His teachings were the foundation of basic language in our own Constitution and Bill of Rights. This was the basis of our society, but I am sure the precepts apply to many countries.

Muhammad

Muhammad was a great man searching for God and had a significant effect on many people, and now his name is honored by a billion followers.

Sir Isaac Newton

Sir Isaac Newton was a key figure in the scientific revolution, so he is my first-world class geek. He helped solidify the concepts of the cosmos and calm the average person's fears of bad things happening. Remember, Einstein and Hawking figure in this too. He discovered the laws of motion and gravitation and was a key figure in the development of optics and calculus. He was the second scientist to be knighted after Sir Francis Bacon.

Aristotle

Aristotle was another geek because he was a great philosopher but also an important fundamental scientist. At age 18 he joined Plato's academy and he stayed 19 years. Powerful duo! Both figured heavily in establishing Western philosophy. He studied biology, zoology, physics, and geology. He is credited with the earliest study of logic and of how things work in the natural world. Today we are more about following the scientific method, which he helped establish, but he also used human intelligence and logic to figure things out.

Leonardo da Vinci

Leonardo da Vinci was another incredibly talented geek, known for his sketches and paintings (Mona Lisa, The Vitruvian Man, and The Last Supper), sculpture (David and Horse), architecture (bridges and movable barricades), and inventions (a flying machine, pumps, and cannons). He needed to have steady work to produce cash flow to live, and then he worked on things as they were needed or as they interested him. I see him as an idea man, a go-to guy when you needed to solve a puzzle or problem.

Albert Einstein

Albert Einstein, from a world view, was all about how this world and the cosmos worked. My favorite quote is, "I am enough of an artist to draw freely upon my imagination. Imagination is more important than knowledge. For knowledge is limited to all we now know and understand, while imagination embraces the entire world and all there ever will be to know and understand." Remember my son saying everything is art? I think Einstein would agree. Here he calls himself an artist—not a physicist or mathematician.

Galileo

Galileo Galilei was another great mind and geek who was involved in the scientific revolution. He was the son of a well-known musician who was fascinated by math and physics. He supported himself mainly from teaching. Notable was his challenge of the old world view of Aristotle and the Catholic Church, supporting the Copernican theory that the Earth and planets went around the sun instead of vice versa. He helped refine the telescope, which assisted his efforts as an astronomer. His modest inventions were used to spot ships, then look at the moon and stars, and eventually led to the Hubble Space Telescope, which is pulling together space data from the dawn of time. Very cool. My favorite quote is, "Passion is the genesis of genius."

Plato

Plato was Socrates' student in ancient Greece. He was a giant in Western civilization founding the Academy in Athens (the first college-style institution) and being so skilled in philosophy and math. The school of thought called Platonism reflected his views. It is said that if you were to write a book on European philosophy, it would have numerous quotes from Plato. My favorite is, "Do not train children to learning by force and harshness, but direct them to it by what amuses their minds, so that you may be better able to discover with accuracy the peculiar bent of the genius of each." This reflects my belief that we are all unique like snowflakes, and that each has a creative genius in them.

Charles Darwin

Charles Darwin was English, not Italian or Greek for a change. He made his living as a geologist and naturalist and is best known for his Theory of Evolution. His five-year voyage on HMS Beagle gave him hands-on experience and credibility in the scientific community. He observed that the struggle for existence led to a branching pattern of evolution (remember my mini-max theory?) where nature chooses the easiest way to survive. The stumbling block for him was his insistence that all creatures come from common ancestry. Well, he did call it his Theory of Evolution, not Facts of Evolution. My favorite quote is, "A man who dares to waste one hour of his time has not discovered the value of life."

Alexander the Great

Alexander the Great is also known as Alexander the Macedonian, a Greek ruler notable for what he did in a very short period of time. He was taught by Aristotle (one of the greats) until age 16. He took over the Kingdom of Macedonia from his father at age 20 and spent most of the rest of his 33 years building the largest empire in the ancient world. Through him, Greek culture and stability spread. My favorite quote gets back to my idea of humanity being sheep or wolves, but he inserted lions for wolves: "I am not afraid of an army of lions led by a sheep. I am afraid of sheep led by a lion." I'm glad we had nurds as a buffer.

Socrates

Socrates was a Greek philosopher who taught Plato. Both were pillars of Western civilization. His name was given to the Socratic Method of breaking down moral or ethical issues into discreet units and answering the little questions to arrive at the big picture. This tactic was also useful in establishing the scientific method. He depended on his love of wisdom to get him through life while acknowledging, "I do not fancy I know what I do not know." He was aware of his own ignorance—a thought that is hopefully valuable to us all. Later in his life this gadfly (a fly that stings the horse into action) was found guilty of corrupting the minds of youthful Athenians and not believing in Greek gods. He was sentenced to death by drinking poison herbs including hemlock. I mentioned my favorite quote from him in my opening: "The unexamined life is not worth living."

Nikola Tesla

Nikola Tesla was a Croatian engineer and inventor. Einstein was a genius but had support from his intelligent wife and assistant. Edison was bright but had lots of help (in the form of Edison Machine Works). Tesla was pretty much on his own and accomplished much. Some say he was "the smartest man who ever lived" and back it up with his over 270 patents. Bold words when Edison and company had over a thousand, but again Edison had help and Tesla was a loner. He focused his efforts in the development of electrical power and electrical devices. He worked for Edison in New Jersey from 1882 to 1886. There definitely was a "war of currents"—Edison promoting DC power and Tesla AC power. History shows that Tesla and AC won that war, so maybe there is some form of justice for Tesla. He said, "I don't care that they stole my idea. I care that they don't have any of their own." Tesla was brilliant and a showman, sometimes acting like what we now call a mad scientist. He found his niche and lived his dream. Now the whole world uses AC power to light their homes and factories. He never married and lived in New York City hotels most of his life. He died alone in room 3327 of the New Yorker Hotel.

Siddhartha Gautama

Siddhartha Gautama, known by most as the Buddha, lived in the foothills of the Himalayan Mountains around 400 BCE. He was a wise man whose name, Buddha, means "enlightened one." His millions of followers still look for their nirvana (end of time). Favorite quote: "Your purpose in life is to find your purpose and give your whole heart and soul to it."

Moses

Moses was a former Egyptian prince later turned prophet, religious leader, and lawgiver. Many believe he wrote the Jewish Torah. He is particularly important to the "big three" monotheistic religions—Judaism, Christianity, and Islam. His face is even a marble relief sculpture in the US House of Representatives. Most agree he was a founder of ancient cities, established a religion and tabernacle, and issued laws (two tablets with the Ten Commandments on them). I see a tie-in to the idea of sheep and wolves. Baby Moses was spared from the wolf Pharaoh by Pharaoh's daughter. Mature Moses led the Hebrew people like sheep out of the mouth of Pharaoh.

Moses knew his shortcomings. He told the Lord, "I am not eloquent…I am slow of speech, and of a slow tongue" (Exodus 4:10), but asked for help: "shew me now thy way, that I may know thee" (Exodus 33:13). The world could use more humble people who are not afraid to ask for help.

George Washington

George Washington must have been a good example of a founding father to people around the world to make the list. He was the first president of a country that in 250 years accounts for half the created wealth of all mankind—pretty incredible. Some of his quotes tie back to some of my ideas: "If freedom of speech is taken away, then dumb and silent we may be led, like sheep to the slaughter." He was also worried about sheep. Another one of his quotes: "The harder the conflict, the greater the triumph"—so don't be afraid of a tough fight. I think his quote, "It is better to be alone than in bad company," is particularly relevant in the age of social media. And another favorite: "It is impossible to account for the creation of the universe without the agency of a Supreme Being."

Confucius

Confucius or Kong Qiu was a Chinese teacher and philosopher who lived around 550 BCE. He championed strong family loyalty, ancestor worship, respect of elders by their children and of husbands by their wives. He espoused the principle "Do not do to others what you do not want done to yourself," a parallel of the Golden Rule. He said he was a "transmitter who invented nothing"—a nice change from Edison and Tesla. Study and schooling were very important to him. He, like Buddha, was a mild man seeking to speak the truth and improve the lives of those he touched. Notable quotes include "Real knowledge is to know the extent of one's ignorance," "Everything has beauty, but not everyone sees it," and "Choose a job you love, and you will never have to work a day in your life."

Mahatma Gandhi

Mahatma Gandhi was the 19th century leader of the Indian independence movement away from British rule. *Mahatma* means "high-souled" or "venerable" and was a title of honor given to him. He was also known as *Bapu* or "father." I mentioned him earlier in the teachings of Jesus because non-violence was core and civil dis-obedience to governing rule was key. In the United States, revolu-tionaries protested a British tax on tea, which led to the Boston Tea Party. In India, Gandhi led protests of the British salt tax. It brought people together. Like George Washington, in India Gandhi is con-sidered the father of the nation. Notable quotes include, "An eye for an eye only ends up making the whole world blind," "Live as if you were to die tomorrow. Learn as if you were to live forever," and, "A man is but the product of his thoughts. What he thinks he becomes."

William Shakespeare

William Shakespeare has the intimidating title of the great-est writer in the English language. He lived in England in the 16th century and made his living writing and acting in plays. The plays he wrote have been translated into every major living language so his thoughts and ideas are in most civilized nations. He set the bar rather high for authors that followed. Some quotes from him include, "We know what we are, but know not what we may be," "It is not in the stars to hold our destiny but in ourselves," and "This above all; to thine own self be true."

Johannes Gutenberg

Johannes Gutenberg lived in 15th century Germany. He made his living like my great-grandfather in Iowa as a blacksmith but also became a goldsmith, printer, and publisher. His contribution to society was the creation of the movable type printing press. Until then every document was done by hand, which took a lot of time and only the church or the very wealthy could afford it. One of his copies of the Old Testament sold for $5.1 million in 1987. Of course that is not the original price but shows its rarity. It is the technology that is important because the printing press dramatically brought the cost and speed of printing down. Basic economics: the more your print, the smaller the unit cost, and hopefully that is passed on to the consumer. Now you can buy a whole Bible at Dollar Tree for $1.00 and can get free excerpts at the Christian Dollar Store. Some call Gutenberg the Steve Jobs (father of the technology for personal computers and smart phones) of his day.

Abraham Lincoln

Abraham Lincoln we discussed a little in Chapter Five. He was a man of the people and very courageous. Have you ever taken a later photo of the President and divided it in half length wise down his nose? The two halves differ greatly just like the divided nation he served. One side looks almost okay while the other very troubled. Much like many of our lives, right? He was self-taught, self-motivated, and in charge of a nation when more Americans were killed than all the other wars combined. He used the technology of the day to create the first Presidential War Room and brought the states into a United States, finally.

Henry Ford

Henry Ford was also in Chapter Five. He took the first step in revolutionizing transportation. The Wright brothers took the second big step. Ford took us from horse and buggy to the automobile. Road technology and signage had to catch up, but he increased conveyance speed from 4 miles per hour to 40 miles per hour. The technology of the assembly line is applied to worldwide manufacturing and has dramatically reduced cost and increased speed like the printing press. I estimate that 10 percent of the US workforce is now employed in manufacturing, selling, fixing, or supporting the automobile business. That is huge.

The Wright Brothers

The Wright brothers took the second big step in transportation by inventing and building the first successful airplane. These brothers were what I call techies, or tinkerers. They were into bicycles, motors, and even printing presses. Like many of us, they were trying to see if they could make a living doing what they loved. They hoped for huge returns with aircraft, so they concentrated on that which ended up revolutionizing their lives and ours. They went from Ford's 40 miles per hour to 400 miles per hour and faster. Now we have rocket sleds at Holloman Air Force Base in New Mexico where on April 30, 2003 they set the world speed record of 6,416 miles per hour.

Bill Gates

Bill Gates is not on the original list. He was a college drop-out. What is important is that he was a technical geek who found a niche—creating a decent operating system—to make a "computer" functional. It ended up being a worldwide phenomenon that made both him and Steve Jobs very rich. He, like Steve Jobs, was no Mr. Nice Guy. "That's the stupidest thing I ever heard," is a quote from him. Gates is not a mini-max person; he worked really hard, wasn't afraid to ask dumb questions, and fought to make sure he was not mischaracterized. It is said he describes himself as a "nerd"—of course I prefer "nurd." Through their foundation, Bill and Melinda Gates have a worldwide effort to help people lead productive and healthy lives. The fruits of their technology translate into food, clothing, and shelter for disadvantaged people. That includes millions of insecticide-treated mosquito nets to prevent malaria.

James Watt

James Watt was a Scottish inventor whose tweaking of the steam engine helped facilitate the industrial revolution, which benefited the whole world. Homeschoolers will be delighted to know that Mr. Watt was mostly schooled at home by his mother, a well-educated woman. He also was a tinkerer, fixing scientific instruments used at the University of Glasgow. That job helped him befriend chemist Joseph Black and the famous Adam Smith. His new ideas for efficient steam engines came when he was asked to work on a university model Newcomen engine. He noticed that it was losing a lot of steam so came up with a new steam condenser to reduce waste. Lesson? Don't be afraid to get your hands dirty. It's honest work and maybe something great will come of it.

Steve Jobs

Steve Jobs is one of two people on my lists that I actually met and talked to briefly. My brother Frank somehow was able to get an early Apple Macintosh computer for me. It was revolutionary technology at the time. I used it to organize personal stuff and for business. Steve Jobs and at least one other business associate were on one of my many cross-country airline flights. He was intrigued when his associate told him he heard me talking about my new Macintosh computer. He wanted to know how I got it, what I used it for, and if I had any ideas on how to make it better or more user friendly. His final question was who was the smartest engineer I knew. He asked me to write down his name and a phone number if I had one and then give it to "the other guy" who was next to him—his associate. He seemed focused and preoccupied, but that's okay. It's always cool meeting someone who was then a definite up and comer who was working hard to make his dream come true. His company, Apple Inc., is a bright light in the technology sky. He moved the goalposts way back on personal computers, phones, and tablets so that the whole world benefits. How many companies put out products and have people sleep on the sidewalk to be in line to get the newest edition? I wish to be so fortunate. He would agree with the old Wayne Gretsky hockey quote, "I skate to where the puck is going to be, not where it has been."

Alan B. Shepard, Jr.

Alan B. Shepard, Jr. is the second world changer I actually met. It was the summer of 1961, and I was visiting my aunt and uncle in the Northeast. There was an on-base celebration for then-Captain Shephard who, on May 5, 1961, flew the Mercury-Redstone 3 (Freedom 7) spacecraft. He was the second man in space after the Russian cosmonaut Uri Gagarin and the first American. The 15-minute ride took him 116 miles up into our atmosphere. It was a very big deal and kicked off the American space program. Then in February, 1971, Shepard was the fifth and oldest American to walk on the moon with Apollo 14. He greeted me and my uncle, said a few kind words, gave me a signed photo and moved down the line. The reason this was significant to me is that it helped me understand the importance of all the school courses in my path. Yes, I was always good in math and science, but sometimes it's hard to understand why they are essential in your schooling. Many industries rely heavily on math and science and luckily they usually pay very well. You should consider them.

Gene Roddenberry

Gene Roddenberry lived the techie/nurd dream. Like Colonel Sanders, it took a while for him to hit his stride. He was a combat pilot in the Air Force during Word War II and a commercial pilot after that. He was a hero copilot on a Pan Am flight from Calcutta to New York. It crashed and he helped save many passengers. In a soul-searching moment he decided to make a career change and followed his father into the LA police force. It was there he started writing TV scripts. The big deal for him was *Star Trek* in 1966, for three TV seasons. That led to the *Star Trek* franchise of 700 episodes and a dozen feature films. The whole world knows the Starship Enterprise and "to boldly go where no man has gone before." Our job is to follow our own plan, our dream and see where it goes. That is our "Enterprise."

Steven Spielberg

Steven Spielberg is a baby boomer born in Ohio to an electrical engineer father who was involved in developing computers. Steven started making films in his early teens (remember the film *8MM*?—that happened to be his early medium). At 13 he won an award for *Escape to Nowhere*. His independent film called *Firelight* was a precursor for *Close Encounters of the Third Kind* and only cost $500 to make, a far cry from the Indiana Jones films later that cost $45 to $70 million. His production company is named after his 1968 short film, *Amblin*. He has made good choices with scripts and actors but the road has not been easy. He has overcome dyslexia, divorce, and anti-Semitism and emerged as one of the greatest filmmakers in cinema history. He followed his dream and entertained us with *Jaws, King Kong, Superman, Indiana Jones*, and *ET.* He educated us with *The Color Purple, Schindler's List*, and *Saving Private Ryan*. One other tidbit. He is an avid video gamer and been involved in producing and developing video games since the 1990s. Thanks, Mr. Spielberg, for raising the bar on quality and content that the whole world is still enjoying.

Chapter Seven: World Changing Females

I am anxious to discuss the resourceful ladies in history. They are important on so many levels. I am convinced that if birth and childcare were left to men, Earth's population would be one tenth of what we see today. I have to admit some difficulty in narrowing the scope of this chapter to lady nurds. If you look for important women in history they are plentiful, but I am looking for inventors, techies, and just plain extraordinary women. If you don't know it by now, I am a history buff although my schooling is in engineering, math, and finance. I'll do my best to do justice to what I have discovered.

The Queen of Sheba

The Queen of Sheba lived during the time of Solomon (also called Jedidiah 990–931 BC). Solomon's wisdom and wealth attracted people from all over the world and many requested an audience. The Queen of Sheba put together a caravan of over 20 camels laden with over $100 million worth of gold, jewels, and spices. She got what she wanted, which was an audience with Solomon, and left with more wealth and a son who would be named Menelik, the father of the dynasty known as Ethiopia. That ended with Haile Selassie in 1974. The queen was resourceful and focused to benefit her family and her people. Check out the possibility of either the real Ark of the Covenant or a copy given by Solomon being there in Ethiopia. I wish the government would allow someone to go in and report back to the rest of us.

Cleopatra

Cleopatra was no second fiddle. She lived from 69–30 BC and became Queen of Egypt at age 17 or 18. She was the last major pharaoh of Egypt (her son Caesarian survived for a short time). At the time it was a major inconvenience to be a woman and a ruler so she had to live by her wits. She spoke nine languages. She used her charm and intellect to survive and keep her empire. Closely aligning with the Roman Empire helped a lot. Her name survives today and her image is on many products.

Joan of Arc

Joan of Arc (1412–1431) got a lot done in her 19 years. She is a national French hero who, in the Hundred Years' War, led the resistance to the English invasion. At 13 years old, she had a vision of Saint Michael, Saint Catherine, and Saint Margaret who told her to drive out the invading English troops. At 16 she cut her hair and with local people's support dressed as a male soldier (one of the first famous "cross dressers") to go see the king. Her charisma, conviction, and energy were a rallying point for the French victory. She saved her country and was later declared a saint. Not bad for a teenager.

Queen Elizabeth I

Queen Elizabeth I (1533–1603) was the last Tudor monarch, also called the Virgin Queen or Good Queen Bess. The current Queen of

England is Elizabeth II. Elizabeth I served as queen from age 25 until her death at age 70. Through all the drama, religious furor, and wars she piloted the English ship well. She spoke seven languages and was a good negotiator. Historians call her tenure a Golden Age. Remember, he or she who has the gold makes the rules…even in politics.

Susanna Wesley

Susanna Wesley (1669–1742) is known as the Mother of Methodism because two of her sons (John and Charles Wesley) were alpha Methodists. She homeschooled her children—nine died as babies and ten survived. She had a lifelong struggle with money because her husband didn't make much and she had so many mouths to feed. Add to that her house burned down twice. Ms. Wesley ended up writing meditations and comments on the Bible to make extra money. She was a great role model because she struggled and endured.

Emilie du Chatelet

Emilie du Chatelet (1706–1749) was a true geek. She was a French mathematician, author, and physicist. Besides being a great role model for other women, she also translated Isaac Newton's works into French so other scientists could reflect on them. Voltaire said of her, "A great man whose only fault was being a woman." Kind of insulting, but you get the point.

Peggy Shippen-Arnold

Peggy Shippen-Arnold was the second wife of Benedict Arnold who didn't see the Revolutionary War as winnable, so she encouraged her husband to sell military information to the British and then defect back to Great Britain. You probably know "the rest of the story from Paul Harvey," but it did not end well for General Arnold and his wife was never punished. As a matter of fact, she kept her wits and was granted 100 pounds sterling per year for life by Queen Charlotte…and then an additional 350 pounds per year from King George III "for meritorious service." Kind of a weird twist in American history that I thought was noteworthy. She survived among the wolves and wasn't a sheep.

Betsy Ross and Mary Pickersgill

Two other women from the Revolution who are talked about are Betsy Ross and Mary Pickersgill. Betsy Ross was a patriot and one of several flag-makers in the Philadelphia area. She has been presented as a role model and a significant contributor to American history. The truth is that she probably did not make the famous flag presented to General George Washington as portrayed in paintings. The design was probably by a committee of several men, including Francis Hopkinson. Yes she was a flag-maker, but so was Rebecca Young, who was documented to have made the Grand Union Flag and Union Jack of the Continental Army. Ross's daughter Mary Young Pickersgill did make the famous Star Spangled Banner with 15 stars and stripes that flew over Fort McHenry in Baltimore during the War of 1812. You can connect the dots to songwriter Francis Scott Key seeing it and writing our National Anthem, "The Star Spangled Banner."

Marie Curie

Madame Marie Curie (1867–1934) is my second female nurd. She was a French physicist who was the first woman to earn a PhD in Europe. Her work led to the discovery of radioactivity and of the elements polonium (named after her beloved Poland) and radium. She won the Nobel Prize not once but twice—first for Physics in 1903 and then for Chemistry in 1911. She is remarkable in that she stepped boldly into the man's world of science. Unfortunately, they did not have the knowledge about effects of chemicals and radioactivity on the human body, so she had an early death.

Amelia Earhart

Amelia Earhart lived about the same time as Madame Curie. Instead of science, she boldly stepped into the man's world of aviation. She was homeschooled with her sister and later wrote books about her flying experiences. She is best known for two things: first, for being the first woman to fly solo across the Atlantic Ocean; second, in 1937 for being lost over the Pacific Ocean while attempting to become the first human (man or woman) to fly around the world. She helped form The Ninety Nines, an organization for female pilots that continues strong to this day.

Madame C.J. Walker

Madame C.J. Walker (real name Sarah Breedlove) also lived in this time frame (1867–1919). She sold cosmetics door to door. Perhaps you are wondering, "What is the big deal about that?" Well, she became the first woman of any color to work her own way to becoming a self-made millionaire. She was born in Louisiana during the time of slavery. Her parents and older siblings were plantation slaves. She was the first child born free after Lincoln's Emancipation Proclamation was signed into law. Determined to make her own way and provide for her daughter, she learned about hair care from her three brothers who were barbers in St. Louis. She moved to Denver to start her own business training what she called "beauty culturists" to consult and sell her products. She rewarded her employees who had good sales, who brought in new culturists (the beginnings of multi-level marketing), and who gave the most to community charities.

Susan B. Anthony

Susan B. Anthony is noteworthy as the most powerful organizer for women's rights in the 19th century. She died in 1906. She and Elizabeth Cady Stanton struggled long and hard for women's right to vote, but Ms. Anthony also was interested in getting rid of slavery and in temperance (control of alcohol). She travelled a lot, giving 75 to 100 speeches per year. Finally, the Anthony Amendment or 19th Amendment to the US Constitution was passed in 1920, giving women the right to vote. And in 1979 she was the first nonfictional woman put on a US coin, the 1979 US dollar.

Clara Barton

Clara Barton (1821–1912) lived in the same time frame as Susan Anthony. My daughter calls her an RN like herself because she actively treated the sick and dying Union soldiers on battlefields of the Civil War. They called her "the Angel of the Battlefield." She never married, so she had to support herself. She went on to Washington DC and might have been the first woman to hold a federal government job at the US Patent Office. The Red Cross actually was begun in Europe around 1860. Its representatives are sent to assist where there are wars, health issues, or natural disasters. Ms. Barton formed a link and founded what is now the American Red Cross and was its first president. Also of note is she wrote an autobiography called *The Story of My Childhood*.

Elizabeth Blackwell

Let's go from nurse to doctor. Elizabeth Blackwell (1821–1910) was the first woman to get a medical doctorate in America. Her sister Emily was the third. Very independent and competitive, she was tired of male domination, so she founded a female medical school in London in 1874. It was called the London School of Medicine for Women. You can read about her view of life and accomplishments in her autobiography entitled *Pioneer Work*. One of life's lessons for me is that if you want to be a pioneer, you often take the arrows. Dr. Blackwell confirms that.

Ella Fitzgerald

Ella Fitzgerald (1918–1996) was a one-of-a-kind jazz singer. During her life she won 14 Grammies and the Presidential Medal of Freedom.

Indira Gandhi

Indira Gandhi (1917–1984) was a world leader, named Woman of the Millennium by the BBC in 1999. She was the third Prime Minister of India and the only woman. Sadly, she was assassinated in 1984.

LaDonna Harris

LaDonna Harris (1931–) is the President and Founder of Americans for Indian Opportunity very much devoted to developing economic opportunity for her multi-tribal Native American organization. She fights for women's rights, civil rights, environmental protection, and societal peace. Her autobiography is called *LaDonna Harris—A Comanche Life.*

Grace Hopper

My first female computer nurd is Grace Hopper (1906–1992). She invented one of the first usable computer languages, which eventually led to the COBOL language. She rose to the rank of Rear Admiral in the US Navy and earned the nickname "Amazing Grace." She popularized the term "debugging," which came from actually removing a moth from a computer. She earned masters and PhD degrees in Math from Yale and is the only person on my list who has a US Navy ship named for her—the USS Hopper (DDG-70). I served three years on USS Cochrane (DDG-21), so I have much respect for her.

Dolores Huerta

Dolores Huerta is a Latina woman who helped create the National Farm Workers Association, which became the UFW, United Farm Workers. She is a tireless champion for social justice, a wonderful role model for Latinos, and worthy of the ballads and murals about her and her life.

Rosa Parks

Rosa Parks stepped into American history on December 1, 1955 as a 42-year-old black woman who refused to give up her bus seat to a white passenger. She was arrested in Montgomery, Alabama for civil disobedience. She became "the first lady of civil rights." The case is legal history. The bus is on display at the Henry Ford Museum in Dearborn, Michigan—an incredible museum. She wrote her autobiography, called *My Story.*

Shirley Ann Jackson

Shirley Ann Jackson is perhaps my favorite female nurd. She earned the first PhD for an African American woman at MIT in nuclear physics. She has been active in education, science, and public policy. She was the head of the United States Nuclear Regulatory Commission where she stressed safety and public health. I hope she writes her autobiography someday.

Helen Keller

Helen Keller deserves note as a survivor of early childhood disease that left her deaf, mute, and blind. She went on to become a noted author and lecturer for others who had similar disabilities. She was the first blind and deaf person to earn a BA degree in the US. Her favorite causes were women's voting, world peace, socialist rights, and rights for people with disabilities. She wrote *My Religion* and then *Light in My Darkness.*

Victoria Woodhull

Victoria Woodhull (1838–1927) was the first woman to be nominated and campaign for the US Presidency by the Women's National Equal Rights Party. She lost but made her statement. She and her sister were the first two female Wall Street stock brokers.

Sally Ride and Ellen Ochos

Dr. Sally Ride and Ellen Ochos were both astronauts. Dr. Ride was the youngest astronaut to orbit the Earth and the first American woman in space. Ellen Ochos was part of the crew of the first shuttle mission in 1993 as a mission specialist conducting studies on solar and atmospheric issues. She was a researcher on advanced optical info systems.

So where are we in this adventure? Being male or female is not the deciding factor in your life. Both can do and have done well. And those mentioned here are not the mini-max type—you remember, minimum effort-maximum result. They worked hard and their success came from making the most of what they either earned or achieved. They did this in their time and their society's rules.

Chapter Eight: Shaping Your Dream

So now you've seen achievers from America and the world, what common themes do you see? Adversity is OK. Getting your hands dirty is OK. Making a living is OK, but don't give up on your dream. These individuals have laid the groundwork for us to build on. Yes there is still room for innovation and "what's next."

For example, I saw a Pennzoil ad for new engine oil made from natural gas. It turns out that the US is now the largest natural gas producer in the world. Some comes from the normal process of drilling for oil where you get some natural gas too. You can also drill just for natural gas. Natural gas is being obtained from the fracking business that is booming in Pennsylvania and elsewhere and is creating tens of thousands of jobs. If you have lots of a raw material (natural gas) then it makes sense to look for other things that you can do with it. How about a new, better quality, longer lasting engine oil? Makes sense. So kudos to the engineers at Pennzoil for their new platinum product.

Information is the driver of technology and business. In my younger days I was the product manager for a high tech business venture funded by a major corporation. They invested millions into new technology to make metals that would hopefully pay off big time. We had a Japanese partner to help market into Asia with a steady stream of visitors. They would come in groups, which I finally figured out were teams usually of three people. There was always a gray haired, dignified looking man who did not speak English. The other two, always younger, men were tasked with writing stuff down and translating from English to Japanese. During their visits one younger man would be asking me questions and translating back to the older man and the other younger man was furiously writing everything down. It was always intense. Then at the end there would be something they did not understand, so they would ask if they could see the plant or processing machinery to clear it up. What they wanted from the very beginning was to see the production line and the plant. Who knows what they would then memorize, write down, or sneak a photo. So my answer was always "No" to going behind the closed and locked production doors.

On one occasion I was quietly sitting in a bathroom stall at work, doing my business, and the Japanese team came in not knowing I was there. Amazingly enough, the older man started talking about the previous night's New York Yankees game, speaking perfect English. Maybe it was the perfect resonance off the tiles like singing in the shower, but I doubt it. Just part of the total picture of them trying to get as much competitive information as possible to take home to build their own business. I don't blame them for trying. After all they did not say out loud that the boss did not speak English, but he only spoke Japanese in my presence and one younger man acted as translator. They were doing what they could to gain competitive information to further their business.

What about you in today's world? Well, you have the Internet, which is a huge source of information and raw material. You don't need to fly from Japan to New York to get much of what you need. The important stuff is probably the "intellectual information" anyway. So the technical people would be a resource. You can research patents, which have a lot of information. Just remember though that many people do not file for patents because it is a link to their competitive information. They have an idea and are running with it hoping to be first in the marketplace and gain market share that others after them will have to fight for. Maybe a technical piece of the product will have patents surrounding it, but the main idea is providing a service or product that many people will want and buy.

So how do you get to this stage in your life where you have this idea for a service or product? Go back to Chapter Two where I talk about influencers. If you talk to my children they will tell you how important I think having a plan is. It guides what I call your "dailies"—what you do on a daily basis. So you have a thought as to what you should do. With our world getting more competitive and more compartmentalized, a basic building block is a good education. So at a minimum go to and finish high school. One of my friends wants his children to choose a career path early and takes them to a VoTech (Vocational Technical) school nearby where they can concentrate on that course of study. For others the general subjects of high school are OK and, after all, that is the most common path to college. I like the idea of VoTech because if you don't want to be a doctor, lawyer, or teacher maybe a trade is OK. I remember the electrician who wired my house drove a fairly new Mercedes coupe, which was kind of embarrassing next to my Toyota Camry. Oh well.

I also know from business that industry is crying for tradesman—especially men and women who are willing to be out and about like a lineman, pipefitter, or welder. In Pennsylvania they are bringing in men from Mexico with no skills, training them for oilfield jobs, and paying them $80,000 per year. If they become skilled as pipefitters, rig operators, etc. it can go over $100,000. That's not bad for no degree and no experience.

So first is education, and don't be afraid of homeschooling. There is one family in the rural Northwest where all the children were homeschooled and all went to Harvard. Look up Dakota Root from Las Vegas; her father says she was accepted at every Ivy League college in America. Opportunities exist. Your job is to find them. Remember, no one can take away an education or a degree.

Second is your thoughts and dreams. That requires a plan. Like in *Indiana Jones* when looking for the Holy Grail, the old knight surrounded by various cups told him to "choose wisely." Common sense versus intellect. If it's a real dream then you won't care if you start at the bottom. Mark Cuban loved the entrepreneurial spirit of the young woman who took scrap metal from old replacement windows her family had collected, sold the metal for $200, and started her baby shoes and moccasins business. She wasn't looking for a handout but a hand up. So don't be afraid to fail and don't be afraid to get your hands dirty. I pumped gas for a while.

Go for quality not quantity, at least at first. Would you like the iPhone if it failed or fell apart after a month or two? So they got the quality right, and then moved on to quantity. I am very pleased to see Apple rethinking its manufacturing locations and having plants here in the US.

> # Don't be afraid to fail and don't be afraid to get your hands dirty.

In your finished product you need to consider the intellectual property aspect of your idea, so don't forget about copyrights and patents. You might want to talk to an attorney at some point. To start your inquiry it would be good to go to the US Patent Office website to take advantage of the advice and to estimate cost. It takes four to six months for them to even look at your idea.

When talking about cost, I am amazed at the lack of knowledge in the young people I talk to about handling, budgeting, and controlling money. After all, it is another tool in your toolbox but a very important one. Many great ideas die because there is no financing available to support the effort. We, therefore, need to spend some time learning about and appreciating the history and significance of money.

Chapter Nine: Money Matters

This chapter will cover significant financial ground. It's important because if you cannot find your money niche in this life, you won't have quality. That does not mean that you have to be wealthy to be happy. You do, however, need to be secure in your financial situation to move forward each day.

I'm starting with financial concepts and then, hopefully, making them relevant. These are life lessons that my daughter Shannon could use in her life skills classes in high school. In economic terms we are going from macro (big scale) to micro (small scale). I'm using mini-max on a complicated subject.

First of all, money is primarily a medium of exchange. In bartering, you exchange one object for another with no money changing hands. Money was created to be a neutral and universal means of buying and selling. Years ago when the United States was getting started there was a big effort to get away from foreign currency or coins. Benjamin Franklin even printed some of the first paper money. Coins were easy. They were silver or gold. Early Roman coins were sometimes bronze. I have an old Spanish *real,* which was later called a piece of eight because owners or merchants would cut them into pieces to do business. At first the paper money was only as good as the state or business that issued it. Eventually, the government stepped in to back their paper money with gold or silver certificates. In 1971 President Nixon took us off the gold standard and allowed the value of our dollars to float with other international currencies. Now the paper money (bills) say, "This note is legal tender for all debts, public or private." No gold or silver backup.

OK, so now you use "cash" or legal paper money to buy stuff, as well as the debit or credit cards that are less likely to carry bacteria or a virus, especially during the COVID pandemic. They are universally accepted. But beware, there are wolves out there looking to steal your money or credit information, using misdirection or fraud. Trust the old saying that if it sounds too good to be true, it usually is.

> # Trust the old saying that if it sounds too good to be true, it usually is.

Check out these four scenarios. First, a Ponzi scheme. Charles Ponzi was a Boston businessman who in 1920 came up with an investment scheme that paid returns to its investors from their own new money or money brought in by subsequent investors. So it's not from profit and not from operations (shows my financial background). Why does it work? Simple—greed. He offered higher returns than other current investments. Abnormally high and unusually consistent while the scheme lasts. The problem for the schemer is the need for an ever-increasing flow of money from new investors. Why does the scheme fall apart? The originator cashes in or disappears, new investment slows down or dries up so he or she cannot keep up payments to current investors, or other factors where investors pull out their money. The most recent convicted felon using this method was Bernie Madoff. In 2009 he pleaded guilty to 11 federal felony counts of defrauding thousands of investors of billions of dollars. He passed away in prison in 2021.

Let's compare that to number two—a pyramid scheme. A Ponzi scheme has one central person who basically knows every investor. He builds their trust and takes advantage of their greed. A pyramid scheme requires recruiting other participants so no one knows all the investors. Ponzi requires some supposed investment or approach and often appeals to the more sophisticated, well-to-do investors. A pyramid is more middle class where you recruit your friends or relatives to bring in new money. That's the source of commissions or fees. Ponzi can go on for years by simply getting the old investors to reinvest their supposed dividends. If that happens, new investors are gravy. A pyramid requires new members and their new money. It will die without them.

Number three is the bubble theory. That means ever rising prices in an open market setting where people or investors notice prices going up (like the 2012–2019 stock market) and they want to get in on it. The other name for this is "the greater fool theory" where you buy an uncertain but attractive investment (like waterfront property, stocks, or bitcoins) in the hope that you can sell it later to someone else; he or she is called the greater fool. Over time the stock market has been good. The bitcoin phenomenon is unique in that it is all digital. Bitcoins are created as a reward for using your computing power on a public, online ledger. Now they are being used for online payments and are traded, hoping that their value goes up. Greater fool, right?

Number four is a challenge for you that I call God's Ponzi scheme.

If the definition of a Ponzi scheme is that the originator knows everyone, that's true—and He promises to bless those who give to Him (that's where the preachers start talking about the tithe) and His cause is dependent on current "investors" giving more or bringing in new "investors." Hmm. Sounds similar to Mr. Ponzi.

However, that's where the similarities end. God does not promise plain "money." He promises blessings. He promises to take care of you and your family's needs, which can come in many forms. The cool thing is that the "scheme" will not die when the originator dies or because investors want to cash out. His investors are worldwide and normally not the well-to-do. As a matter of fact, most of the 2013 individual giving of $240 billion in the US came from below average to average wage households. Check and see how much one rich person gave (a senator/Secretary of State). In 1993 it was about $2,000. In 1994, $175. And in 1995 a big $0. They're doing much better now but it's a good example of how giving is not a high priority for many high profile people. Average Joes give *much* more.

Let me make two statements about being born. First, you were born to be a billionaire. You know how much I like math. Well, if you live to be 30 years old a normal heart muscle will have beaten over one *billion* times. Next, the society you live in makes a huge difference. I tell my friends that being born here or coming to the United States is like winning the lottery. You have the opportunity to live an unfettered life, free from most societal demands. If you work hard you can make enough money to live a comfortable life. And if you don't, there is a huge societal safety net. I saw a program about "being poor" recently. Millions of families and children do not have basic food, clothing, or shelter around the world. The poorest of the poor are in Congo, Niger, Burundi, Mozambique, and Liberia (remember the Ebola plague?). Their average monthly income is about $70 US. In the US it is 50 times that. In Qatar it is 150 times that. In Singapore, Brunai, and Kuwait it is 80 times that.

In the US they asked our "poor," "Do you have a place to live, a car, a TV, and a cell phone?" Most said "yes." Tell someone who makes $70 per month that you are poor. No way.

The incentive is to graduate with no debt or very little debt.

If you decide that college is important, then paying for it is challenging. If you are a student or have children who will be, there are numerous programs to help you. Obviously the best is scholarships or grants where you don't have to pay the money back. I recently told a high school junior about "work colleges" where typically you are required to work 10 to 20 hours per week to dramatically defray college costs. The list includes:

- Alice Lloyd College in Kentucky
- Berea College in Kentucky
- Blackburn College in Illinois
- College of the Ozarks in Missouri
- Deep Springs College in California
- Ecclesia College in Arkansas
- Sterling College in Vermont
- Warren Wilson College in North Carolina.

It helps if you know what you want to study before considering one of these schools, but they will work with you. The incentive is to graduate with no debt or very little debt.

Another more recent college student opportunity is with state run schools. Currently there are seven states with Promise or scholarship programs. The most ambitious is New York State Excelsior Scholarships. This is for initial bachelor degrees in the state university system. It covers tuition and fees—*not* room and board, which sometimes is not cheap. Family income limits are:

- 2017 at $100,000 per year
- 2018 at $110,000 per year
- 2019 at $125,000 per year

The catch is that you must live and work in New York State the same amount of years as your number of years of study. If you do not, it becomes a payback loan.

For two-year community colleges, tuition forgiveness programs include:

- Tennessee Promise at 13 community colleges
- Tennessee Reconnect for ages 24-plus
- Oregon Promise
- Rhode Island Promise
- Minnesota MnSCU Occupational Grant Pilot Program
- Arkansas Grant
- Work Ready Kentucky Scholarship
- Bobcat Promise in Texas
- San Francisco Promise
- Boston Bridge

The main concept here is to minimize your debt. Student loans can be crushing, especially for a young couple. Have you ever listened to the no-debt guru named Dave Ramsey? He and his daughter give seminars and he is on the radio every day here in the New York area. His big thing is to not go into debt for anything except maybe a house. Ever hear of your FICO score? He calls it your debt score. Most lenders look at that as an indication of how well you handle your debt, so if you are going to buy something or apply for a credit card they will look up your FICO score or one of the other two credit report scores. The table is set up from 350 to 850.

- 580 or less is Very Poor
- 580-620 is Poor
- 620-680 is Fair
- 680–720 is Good
- 720–850 is Excellent

So if you are in the high 600s to low 700s you are fairly normal, but don't think getting a credit card or loan is a shoe-in. Many people have to work at improving their credit score before buying a big ticket item. There are even companies that will assist for a fee.

Dave Ramsey is a financial adviser. His nightly show is called *Ramsey Solutions*. He has another way to deal with debt. He says to pay cash for everything except a house—and even a house if you can do it. It reverts back to our grandparents where the thought was if you really want to buy something then save up for it and pay cash.

My best story of this is my old friend John. He grew up in the South and was not educated. He worked with his hands all his life; he never worked for a big corporation with a regular pay check, matching retirement plan, or stock options. He went out almost every day and worked. Even when he had a heart attack in his 50s, the doctor came to his house, diagnosed him, gave him two prescriptions, and told him to lie on the living room couch for six months and let his wife handle most of his needs. Then after six months he was allowed to move upstairs to his own bed. Then after nine months he got clearance to return to work.

John and his wife wanted to buy a small but nice home here in New Jersey. They shopped around for houses out in the country where the property taxes weren't too high. They didn't really care about schools because there were no children in the house. They found a home they liked and agreed to the sale price ($80,000 range) with the owner and avoided paying real estate fees. He was told to show up in a few weeks at the local lawyer's office to pay for the house and sign the appropriate paperwork. He came with his wife and his lunch bag. They signed the necessary paperwork and the lawyer asked how he was paying for the home. John reached for the floor and put his paper lunch bag on the table. "Cash," he said. Everyone's jaw dropped. He was from the old school. If you want something bad enough, save up for it and pay cash.

Dave Ramsey's FICO score is "indeterminate." With no debt and no recent credit history, they don't know how to score him. How can you live like that, you say? You need to have credit, right? The only case I can think of where it is a bit of a problem if you want to pay cash is in renting a car, which is much easier if you have a credit or debit card. Debt is a heavy anchor around your neck (note the nautical term). It limits your options and weighs you down. One of the top three reasons for divorce is money—finances, debt.

I heard of a newly graduated medical doctor here in New Jersey. He had a hard time finding the right job, not because of specialty or personality. He had a big monthly "nut" to crack. He rented an apartment, so that was $1,500 per month. He had a leased car, so that was $350 per month. He had to have heat, electric, and food, so that was $1,000 per month. Now the big one. He had $450,000 in student debt, so that is $4,000 per month. He had to bring in $6,850 per month after taxes to make ends meet. That's a lot of money. By doing some planning, not necessarily going to an Ivy League college or graduate school, and paying cash, people can avoid the debt burden.

Also important here is learning how to say "No." In our internet enhanced society where six-year-olds have their own smartphones, it is a difficult concept. I think of the cartoon called *Peanuts* where Charlie Brown is the main character and he has a friend named Lucy. She does not like being told no—ever. My two cents on the subject is that no is for now, but not necessarily forever. You might want the new Apple iPhone, but yours is working OK and you don't really need the better camera or all glass exterior. And it's $1,000. So that no might be kind of easy. But what about a senior citizen's very tough decision because of limited income—buy food or the medicine the doctor wants you to take. No to food means hunger. No to medicine has medical consequences.

> # True friends are those who make *you* better. They challenge you. They can hold you accountable if you are open to the concept.

Part of the problem is peer pressure from your friends. Take note that many of today's friends will not be there a year or two from now. Their opinions might be relevant to today's business, but definitely not long term. There is no need to be the "-er" or the "-est" of your group. There's no winning in comparisons. There will always be someone richer, smarter, etc. And to shoot for richest is an endless loop where there is no peace or contentment. True friends are those who make *you* better. They challenge you. They can hold you accountable if you are open to the concept. These kind of friends are keepers—hold on to them, maybe for a lifetime.

Chapter Ten: Nurds Today

OK, let's regroup. I have thrown a lot of information at you but I don't want you to "nurd out" on me. So far I wanted you to see where the word *nurd* came from with a detailed history and explanation. Then we walked through history with someone else's list of who was important, and I added my opinion as to why they were important. Remember my discussion about Albert Einstein and the term *Einstein* being used for genius. Well, I would like to think about doing the same and creating the term *Nurd* as one of honor and distinction, not at all like the wacky characters in the movie *Revenge of the Nerds*. Just as Sam Nurdlinger thought of himself and his family as "special," I want nurds to think of themselves and of other nurds as special.

OK, what are nurds today? They are still seen as different. I was watching a movie and one character said to another who did not understand what his techie friend was saying, "That's OK, I speak nerd." In other words, the one guy did not understand the technical terminology. Well, if nothing else I have pointed out the tremendous impact of technology on the economy of the United States and the rest of the world.

World history shows that until the technical age, countries would grow by conquest—more land and natural resources. I would be so bold as to say that if we did not have the technical nurds in our past, there probably would not be a middle class or at least such a large middle class here in the US. Before 2017 there was employment stagnation, 29-hour work weeks to avoid the Affordable Care Act penalties, wages not going up, many companies doing away with their retirement packages, and banks being very tough in granting home mortgages. The economy was better until the COVID-19 pandemic hit in early 2020. Then the government ordered almost everything shut down. The recovery has been spotty and slow.

If we did not have the technical nurds in our past, there probably would not be a middle class or at least such a large middle class here in the US.

One observation is that the middle class is under assault. I'm not a politician so I am not qualified to render an opinion on what is going on with the seeming "ruling class" in Washington, DC and the revolving door between being a representative or senator and then a lobbyist. It does bother me, though. I would rather spend my time talking about what you can do to "live long and prosper."

Not everyone has skills in math and science. I did and I could have been a medical doctor (like my father and brother-in-law), a scientist, or engineer—which I did pursue. Watching *Shark Tank* on CNBC, I am reminded that there are a lot of people who have genuinely good ideas but need help in developing them. So my overall recommendation to follow what you love still holds true. If you work toward being the best of whatever you choose, you will succeed. I've told dozens of young people not to worry about how crowded the market is for what you choose to do. If you are the best, the cream will always float to the top and you will be OK.

Now that doesn't mean that you will make the same money as the young doctor I cited before who needed $6,000 per month to just meet his basic expenses. I mean that you will be able to make money and live a decent life. If that is not OK, then don't strive to be a butcher, baker, or candlestick maker. I've met many New Yorkers who work in or near New York City who hate the commute, hate their jobs, but love the money. You have to choose what makes you happy and go for it.

If you work toward being the best of whatever you choose, you will succeed.

If by chance you do want to pursue the technical route, then you have a higher probability of making more money. There's also the statistic that if you have a college degree you probably will make $1 million more in your lifetime than someone who does not have a college degree. But it does matter what the degree is in. Don't be the young man I met who was a Harvard graduate. "Oh," I said, "that's impressive. What was your major?" "Renaissance poetry," he said. "And what is your favorite memory of Harvard?" I asked. "I don't really remember too much Mr. Rampton. I was high most of the time." *Very impressive*, I thought. I also wondered how his parents felt about that after spending $200,000 on his education. I wish him well.

Many celebrities don't mind talking about what it was like being nurdy in their childhood. Onthebright.com lists many, such as:

- Demi Moore
- Robert Downey, Jr.
- Ariana Grande
- Dwayne (the Rock) Johnson
- Scarlett Johansson
- Kate Moss
- Channing Tatum
- Eminem
- Ryan Reynolds
- Jennifer Garner

I wonder if they would mind being called nurds today? I probably should ask them. That includes the members of my favorite rock band AlterBridge.

Some celebrities apparently don't mind being labeled nurds at all. On Grunge.com they include:

- Tom Hanks, who loves old typewriters and the sounds they make. His book *Uncommon Type* describes his hobby.
- Natalie Portman is heavily into psychology. She interrupted her career to go back to school. In *The New York Post* she said, "I'd rather be smart than a movie star."
- Rosario Dawson and Ben Stiller are very comfortable being called Trekkies.
- Stephen Colbert is into Tolkien and *Lord of the Rings*, especially the character Gandalf.
- Danica McKellar from *The Wonder Years* loves math and has written books about it. I love the title *Math Doesn't Suck*.
- Rod Stewart loves his model trains. In 2008, *Model Railroader Magazine* talked about his layout called Stewartville.

- Dave Bautista, pro wrestler and star of *Guardians of the Galaxy*, loves vintage metal lunch boxes.

And lastly, two celebs who have their PhDs.

- Dexter (Bryan) Holland of *The Offspring* loves molecular biology. His thesis was "Discovery of Mature Micro RNA Sequences...." Too complex for me.
- Bryan May of Queen has his PhD in Astrophysics. Maybe he can help with the giant rock headed near Earth in 2029 called Apophis, the Egyptian god of chaos. End-timers might want to check it out.

> Note: if any of the above celebs want to give me some feedback, please email me at info@alphanurd.com. My son Steve or my nephew will get back to you. We might even put together a "Notable Nurds" book or section on the website.
>
> If you're not a celebrity and want to be included, I encourage you to write to me at info@alphanurd.com and tell me why you are a "Notable Nurd." Having a heartbeat is not enough; you need a brain and hopefully a kind heart too. Let me know what you're doing, especially if it enriches the lives of your family, friends, and neighbors. Making money is one thing. Improving people's lives quite another. If enough people respond I'll open up NotableNurds.com.

Chapter Eleven: Reality in *Your* Plan

T here are some great role models out there, both male and female. Rush Limbaugh said he was the "mayor of realville." I like that because we don't live in a fantasy. Being real with yourself is important. If you are like my wife and can't stand the sight of blood, you probably should not be a surgeon. If you are not good at math and science, then engineering is out. If you love animals then consider being a vet. If you want to make a lot of money, play the lottery—*no*, only kidding.

Being real with yourself is important.

The world we live in works around supply and demand (basic economic terms). Society is willing to pay you for your skills if it needs them. For example, there are thousands of technical jobs available today but not enough qualified applicants. Remember my example of the immigrant working in the Pennsylvania oil fields? They needed workers so desperately they hired him, trained him, and paid him $75,000-plus. Doesn't do much good to have a BA in Renaissance poetry from Harvard unless you want to teach or write. Guidance counselors often recommend a series of tests called Career Aptitude Testing. The Princeton Review has a quick one at www.princetonreview.com/quiz/career-quiz. MAPP Career Assessment is good. In high school you can try www.yourfreecareertest.com.

The trump card is passion for an activity that could develop into a career. The medical doctor who knew she wanted to be a doctor from age six has a big advantage over the undecided masses. In *October Sky* (the 1999 film), Homer H. Hickam, Jr. is a coal miner's son living in Coalwood, Alabama who wanted to study rocketry and eventually become a NASA engineer.

My own son Steve, a brilliant student who was always on the honor roll and dean's list, has loved art since a young age. Because of my US Navy contacts, I had a link to get him into the Naval Academy at Annapolis, but he said "no thanks." Then he was awarded a four-year NROTC scholarship to any university in the US with an NROTC program (like Vanderbilt). Not interested. In frustration I kind of harshly asked him, "What *do* you want to do?" "I want to be an artist," he said. My response was that the Vatican is not hiring right now. Graphic design seemed logical, but he was good in painting and sculpture too—and very talented in caricatures and cartooning. Long story short, he graduated summa cum laude from Mason Gross School of the Arts at Rutgers and never looked back. Check out his amazing work at Binarygod.com or CaricaturesbySteve.com.

Remember the main tenet of this book is that one person can make a difference? I could list inventors like the 3M guy who stumbled on to the Post-it® Note adhesive or the engineer behind the microwave "radar range." But in my experience it's better to talk about something you know personally. Well, I have a good example for you. It's a little technical, so bear with me.

My friend Lance Renfrow has been in the chemicals business for a half century. I won't get into his resume or the details of his being in the Water Ski Hall of Fame (2012). I want to talk about his discovery/refinement, its dramatic benefit to industry and the environment, and how difficult it is in today's busy business world to introduce a new product.

Allow me to get into the weeds a little. Millions of tons of caustic soda are made each year as a byproduct of making chlorine. It's a decent cleaner and inexpensive, perfect for the stainless steel vessels and tubing in beer brewing, dairy/ice cream/yogurt production, and in ethanol (you know, the octane boosting stuff they add to gasoline). Caustic soda does not wet the metal surfaces very well so they can be cleaned, so Lance invented and patented new technology to dramatically improve wetting, cleaning, and efficiency.

> # It's not enough just to have a new idea. It's got to make dollars and sense to those who will be selling and using it.

There was some fine tuning required, and at one point another friend, Dave Burdette (Allegiance Chemicals), was involved. Check out Chapter 14 for more on him. Lance got beer giant Anheuser Busch to try the product. Now all the Anheuser Busch plants use it along with Sam Adams (Boston Brewing) and a major western Dairyman's Supply Company facility. Sam Adams management must be smiling because their goal was to have the freshest tasting beer in the market. There is no better formulation than Lance's for cleaning out vessels and pipes to get rid of bacteria, improve shelf life, and improve taste. The added benefit is eliminating the final step in using a chlorine chemical blend. The EPA has cracked down on the pulp and paper industry to minimize chlorine use because there is evidence that it breaks down in the environment into dioxin, one of the most poisonous chemicals on Earth. So now they don't need chlorine anymore in breweries and dairies. I realized also that making ethanol from corn is a lot like making beer, so the ethanol producers could benefit greatly from this same technology. My friends at Allegiance were also involved along with Les Suhayada and Cliff Daly/John Mercurio at TR Solutions.

I hope Lance doesn't mind me inferring he is a nurd. This example is useful because it shows we still need nurds—they invent and refine some cool stuff, and it's not always easy to get people or businesses to try it. Also, if you talk to a sales professional the hardest product sell is a new product going to a new customer. Everyone is busy. Technical expertise isn't always there, so it's tough to sell a new idea. Just ask the innovators who have been on *Shark Tank*. It's not enough just to have a new idea. It's got to make dollars and sense to those who will be selling and using it. Right, Sharks?

Once again I am reminded of my conversation with Steve Jobs on the airplane. He wanted to know how I got the Macintosh computer, was it easy to use, for what applications did I use it, did I have any problems with the screen or keyboard, etc. So having a new idea or product is not enough. It's got to be user friendly and saleable. If it's not, "another one bites the dust."

Chapter Twelve: An Examined Life

S ome of us are organized, some not. When we moved from Louisiana to New Jersey, we sold a large home but could only afford a small home in the Garden State. To avoid super high prices I had to find land and be the general contractor for an afford-able house—but that's another story. The point is that our home is small. Our oldest daughter Susanna inherited my organizing DNA. So weekly she is organizing and reorganizing in our house. The benefit for her is that it makes her daily life easier because she is a mom and nurse who often works late, so she doesn't have a lot of free time. By being organized in your personal life it helps you focus on your school or career. It minimizes daily issues and is the foundation on which you can build your life and your career plan.

So what about your plan? Do you have one? It can be open ended at first, like you want to be a plumber like your uncle. Or you want to have that bachelor's degree that many employers require. But then you have to put legs to that plan. Your individual plan needs to have details, which you and your family and counselors should attempt to put on paper. I told my children early that they needed to have a plan. Change it every day if you want, but have a plan.

Why is a plan important? It gives you direction, and that direction guides you to your destination. You could be the fortunate one who knows you want to be an engineer. That means working hard in high school, getting decent grades with some cool extracurriculars, and then applying to three tiers of engineering schools. Top schools should be 10 percent of your applications; middle, 40 percent; lower, 50 percent. You could even do some internships to improve your chances. But what if you don't know what you want to do? Welcome to the majority.

> # Being organized in your personal life helps you focus on your school or career. It minimizes daily issues and is the foundation on which you can build your life and your career plan.

If you were in my family and came to me for plan advice I would say:

1. What do you enjoy doing?
2. What are you good at? (Probably numbers one and two will overlap.)
3. Take the career assessment suggestion in Chapter 11 and see if that helps.
4. If you love working with your hands consider a trade. You already know the story of my electrician and his Mercedes. Start with trade school, then apprenticeship, then licensing.

If you are successful and build your own business, you can take home a *lot* of money.

5. If you want the confidence of having the bachelor's degree that many employers insist on, then consider the eight no-debt colleges or the two-year community college route and advancing to the four-year college. Pick one known for its specialties if you can identify what specialty you desire.

Remember, the cream always rises to the top even if you choose a crowded profession. People notice excellence, so you will rise in that field.

Why is all this important? If you have a plan then you don't have to know all the details of your path. Remember I said there's no such thing as coincidence. With a plan you'll see the pieces of the puzzle fall into place one by one. With the inherent structure of a plan, it will give meaning to your daily life. Later on when you are older and examining your life, you will have fewer regrets.

If you have a plan then you don't have to know all the details of your path.

Psychologically we are pre-wired. By pursuing your dreams you will enhance your feeling of wellbeing. Your self-image and self-worth get a boost, like adrenaline. There's a tie-in between body, mind, and spirit. By using your body and mind you supercharge your spirit and outlook. It will help you gain insight.

Not having a plan could mean lost opportunity. My friend Matt Jones reminded me that the McDonald brothers had a great idea for organizing their Speedee Service System for fast service on hamburgers and fries, but it took Ray Kroc's plan to use their idea and sell or service franchises across the world to get to 38,000 restaurants and a personal fortune.

I have hope that the fundamental idea of having a plan will become more mainstream in academia and the private sector. My wife was watching an episode of *Undercover Boss* when I came home from work. I overheard the CEO of True Value Hardware talking to an underperforming employee. He obviously wanted to help this young man and told him that he needed a life plan. He also offered to be a personal mentor. It was music to my ears.

Your Special Page

This page is for **you.** Write down your thoughts, aspirations, and plans. Use it to help you focus on your ideas and dreams.

1. I enjoy doing:

2. I'm good at:

3. My dreams include:

4. Right now I see the stages of my plan to be:

A.

B.

C.

D.

E.

F.

G.

Remember, have a plan; work the plan; change the plan—but have a plan.

Chapter Thirteen:
"Follow Your Dream"
Story

Y ou'd think that at 73 my life should be pretty much over. Not that I am in the same league, but there are some notable senior citizen exceptions:

- Benjamin Franklin (politics and the Declaration of Independence)
- Colonel Sanders (started Kentucky Fried Chicken at age 65)
- Thomas Edison (lightbulb, phonograph, and much more)

I've started something new with some NFL Legends (that's the new term for retired NFL players).

I have the good fortune of being friends with Lee Rouson, two-time Super Bowl champion with the New York Giants (XXI and XXV). The roots of what we are doing is our love for young people and how tired we are of seeing too many die each year. This can be from accidents, homicides, drug overdoses, or suicide. Bullying is also a problem. Statistics show that the number of deaths of young people under the age of 20 has averaged 16,000 from 1999–2006, but the number of drug overdose deaths has gone from 3,400 in 1999 to 17,000 in 2007 and is growing. These deaths are preventable.

When you mentor someone, you want to see a result. Getting a measurable result requires training and measurement sticks to see if you are going where you want to go with the mentoring. That's what Lee and I are doing, targeting middle and high school students.

On a personal level I see my grandson Isaiah tempted every day with Facebook, YouTube, and games. In our society the ways to escape reality include drugs, video games, virtual reality, and binge watching TV shows. It's so easy to just pick up the tablet, iPod or smartphone and start looking/playing. We monitor what Isaiah is watching, but it's easy to lose track of websites and time. In fairness I must point out that he lives in a somewhat sheltered environment in New Jersey. There are millions of kids just in the United States who wrestle with much worse environments and temptations.

Lee and I have driven a stake in the ground to say this is not OK. In *Lord of the Rings: The Fellowship of the Ring*, Gandalf the wizard decides to confront an ancient demon in Middle Earth. The statement "You shall not pass" rings out, meaning the demon cannot go along the narrow stone bridge over a bottomless canyon to harm his friends Frodo Baggins and Aragorn. He took a stand against this evil personage. Lee and I are doing the same here in the real world.

There's another reason I'm teaming up with Lee. Over a year ago he asked me to drive and accompany one of his NFL friends named Ken Johnson. Ken played one year with the Dallas Cowboys and seven years with the Cincinnati Bengals. I was Ken's gopher for the day. I picked him up and drove him to the Middlesex County VoTech School in New Jersey where he was invited to be a motivational speaker for the roughly 1,800 high schoolers. We arrived and were greeted by the principal and his staff who were very glad to have a former NFL star speak to their students. I had the mandatory NFL player cards and black Sharpie® for Ken to sign autographs.

We were escorted to their large gymnasium where hundreds of teenagers were already assembled to hear Ken speak. His life story is truly inspiring. The young people settled down. The vice principal gave Ken a live microphone. He tapped it, did the usual sound check, and called me over. "Hey Steve, I want you to go first." What? I was his driver for the day. "You have some great stories so share something for about five minutes." I panicked. What could I share that would interest these young people?

Remember what I said: It's better to talk about something or someone you know. Well my wife, nicknamed Noah, and I raised three very different children and one lesson we learned was to let them follow their dreams. *OK*, I thought, *that's what I'll talk about.* Steven Dennis, our son, is pursuing an art career; Susanna is our authoritative nurse, and Shannon is our compassionate teacher. The short speech was well received. The best audience response was from a row of young ladies in front of me. They were very vocal in affirming a quote from Shannon from what I remember to be around 7th grade: "Dad, I hate school." The girls said "Yeah, we hate school too." They looked at each other and giggled.

We all can have a better life if you pay attention to the small things.

So I did my five minutes on "Follow Your Dreams," encouraging the students to go through the process of figuring out who they really are and then follow their dreams to become that person. It isn't easy, but it is very important.

I can't even estimate how many adults I have known who hate their jobs but love the paychecks and weekends to party. Several students came up later to tell me they definitely would follow their dream. Then I introduced Ken. The young people sat up straight and leaned forward to better listen. Wow. There was a kind of twinkle in their eyes as Ken took the microphone. If I noticed it, then I'm sure the staff and principal did also. Yes, Ken is an imposing figure at six feet six inches tall, but he reminded the crowd that he was in the .1 percent of high school senior football players who are drafted into the NFL annually. So out of 10,000 high school football players, that's only 10. His family story is amazing. His college career at Indiana was playing basketball, not football. His NFL stories are great. He emphasized that it is the journey that is important, not just accomplishments. We all can have a better life if you pay attention to the small things. Also important is to avoid making big mistakes because they can ruin your plans and your life. Your parents, guardians, and teachers can help *if* you'll talk to them.

So I saw the spark when the NFL star spoke. Instant respect. I told Lee about it and that the desire of my heart was to reach out and help young people like these high schoolers. He's been active for over 20 years with his "Move Your Chains" program (football analogy). We are calling our new program "The Ship" (www.theshipnj.com and theshipnj@gmail.com). We had our first football youth camp with Lee and Odessa Turner (also a New York Giants alum) in August, 2019. Fifty-five kids attended. They and their parents and guardians were thrilled with the energy and teaching. From that we want to grow a leadership/mentorship program for summer time and after school. One special note on the first camp. At the end Lee, Odessa, and the coaches selected two MVPs (most valuable players). My grandson Isaiah was one. I was very proud of him.

So can one person make a difference? I want to encourage you that yes, one person can. After Ken and I finished our speeches at

Middlesex County VoTech, many students stepped up to speak to Ken and two students came forward to talk to me. One young man told me how much he appreciated my talk and asked for my autograph. All I had were Ken Johnson's cards so I asked Ken to autograph the front and I signed the back. Another junior class member came forward to tell me he always has wanted to be an artist like my son. His teachers told him he had talent, but his mom discouraged him and told him there is no money in art. He needed to take business or technical courses. Well, after that morning he said he was going to speak to her again and hopefully sign up for more art classes to follow that dream. He gave me a hug and waved goodbye. It had a big impact on me.

The mentorship program is next. We're working on it. We want to mix learning/training and fun. Who wouldn't want to have an NFL player teach and perhaps throw the football a little? My friends at the Liebenzell Retreat Center in New Jersey (Liebenzellretreat.org) supplied the field for the football camp and have amazing facilities to accommodate almost any size group, not just football. If you go to the website you can see many photos of the facilities and camp. We plan on making it an annual event.

Chapter Fourteen: Don't Give Up

Do you remember my reference to my friend Dave Burdette in Chapter 11? Well there's more to his story and it centers on not giving up.

Dave was a tall, bronzed superman. Handsome. Athletic. Intelligent. The old saying is all the guys wanted to be like him and all the girls wanted to be with him. All that came crashing down one day as he was riding his bicycle. I don't know the details of the accident, but a car hit and ran over him leaving him for dead in the street. No insurance. No relief. He is paralyzed from the waist down—also called a paraplegic.

It would have been easy for Dave to give up, but he didn't. He and his brother have built Allegiance Chemicals from $0 to over $50 million sales per year. You think it's rough traveling with two good legs, well, imagine trying it on a wheelchair.

I admire Dave for his not giving up both on a personal and professional level. Just think of the obstacles to overcome and then to plan and build a multimillion dollar business. Right now we are working on a project with his manager, ClearSolutionsUSA, and

Naturechem. As I pointed out before, the hardest sale is a new product to a new customer. Well, we have a plan and are working it daily. We've changed it twice but are succeeding. It's a great example that the planning model works and we're not giving up.

Chapter Fifteen: Don't Be Afraid

One person asked me if I consider myself the Alpha Nurd. In a way I am because in many respects I am like the Wikipedia description of a nerd/nurd, but I coined the term to describe and make fun of other people. Even today it's a way of teasing, often in a non-complimentary way. You can't say it enough around me because it describes an important part of who I am. A few weeks ago I corrected a friend named Greg Quinlan who was mistaken about a historical fact. "Nurd," he said. My only response was to smile because he has no idea (till after he reads this) who in the nurd universe he was talking to. He said it to tease me. In other situations it could be hurtful, and I regret that.

In my mind being a nurd is neither good nor bad. It is a descriptive term so use it in a constructive way. Look at all the historical nurds I have pointed out in this book. Be encouraged by their passion "to move the ball forward" as Lee would say. Many of their inventions we take for granted today, but where would we be without them? Just a few are Edison with the lightbulb, Steve Jobs with the personal computer, and his company, Apple, with the iPhone and more.

So be nice to the nurds around you. Don't tease the nurds on the bus. Listen to the nurds at school—they could be your teachers. You don't have to wear the glasses with the bandage in the middle like you see on TV. Your life is precious. As in the Preface I want to inspire you to analyze, plan, and create your own life, your best life. Remember what Socrates said: "The unexamined life is not worth living." Don't be afraid. If you were born in the United States I tell people that they have already won the lottery. There is more opportunity here than anywhere else—perhaps in history. Go. Dream. Make your big plan and then take small steps to follow through on that plan. Be a world changer. You can do it.

> **Be nice to the nurds around you. Don't tease the nurds on the bus. Listen to the nurds at school—they could be your teachers.**

Post Script

Remember in Chapter 1 I mentioned the original nerd came from Dr. Seuss? It was a cool animal creature, not the human nurd I envisioned. Well I had some thoughts on the subject and spoke to my son about it. He came up with his representation of what the cool animal might be.

Meet Mr. Owl Nurd.

Appendix A: Expanded List of Nerd/Nurd Examples

Infosphere.org says that *nerd* is a word used to describe a fan of the show *Futurama*.

Nerdlinger is the name of a punk rock band from Sydney, Australia who are "slowly working their way to liver failure and an early grave" (check out nerdlinger.bandcamp.org).

Nerdtree is a site for navigating complex file systems.

Nerdwax.com is a site that sells a wax to apply to glasses nose pieces to keep them from slipping.

Nerdtears.com is where the upbeat Kevin McCarthy gives a rundown on films and his rating/opinion as to viewing worthiness.

Appendix B: Cognitive Snapshot

O

K. You've seen what I did with "nurd."

I thought it useful to give you two other examples of how my mind works.

I've been thinking about book titles. Alpha Nurd is my first choice but I've considered others. Furst Nurd came to mind. Then Primier Nurd. I got the adjective by combining not two but three other words. I wanted to combine the words "prime" (the best), "primer" (in weapons, it gets the internal explosion going), and "premier" (original and best). So I came up with "primier," pronounced pri-me-er. That's a new word.

In the dictionary, there is a term called *portmanteau* where you combine two words into one. There isn't a term that describes three words into one. So on December 22, 2020 I thought about it and came up with the new word *triwurd—tri* meaning three and *wurd* which is Frisian (area including part of the Netherlands and north-western Germany) meaning word. It also compliments using a "U" in nurd. That's a new word also. Made my day.

I know, "What a nurd!"

Appendix C: Major Historical Advancements

ccording to Big Think 5, the major advancements of world history in chronological order include:

Fire—a man or woman with two sticks (or lightning/volcano)

Wheel—Mesopotamia about 3500 BC

Nails—Egypt, 3400 BC

Optical lenses—Ancient Greece

Compass—China, 300 BC

Paper—China, 100 BC

Gunpowder—China, 800 AD

Printing press—1439

Electricity—roots in ancient Egypt, then Greece, then the 18th century

Steam engine—circa 1170

Internal combustion engine—19th century

Telephone—1876

Vaccinations and pasteurization—circa 1800

Automobile—19th century

Airplanes—20th century

Penicillin—1928

Rockets—ancient China then 20th century

Nuclear fission—20th century

Semiconductor—1940s

Personal computer—1970s

The Internet—1960s

Endnotes

1. Wikipedia, the Free Encyclopedia, s.v. Nerd, https://en.wikipedia.org/wiki/Nerd.
2. Wikipedia, the Free Encyclopedia, s.v. Mi-2/NuRD complex, https://en.wikipedia.org/wiki/Mi-2/NuRD_complex.
3. World English Dictionary, s.v. Nerd, (publisher).
4. Dr. Seuss, *If I Ran the Zoo* (Random House, 1950).
5. "The 100 Most Influential Figures in American History," *The Atlantic*, Atlantic Media Company, December, 2006, https://www.theatlantic.com/magazine/archive/2006/12/the-100-most-influential-figures-in-american-history/305384/.

About the Author

S teve Rampton is a former US Navy officer who has a love for both words and history. He has a BA from Vanderbilt University and an MBA from Tulane University. Currently, he works with NFL players to encourage young people to follow their goals and dreams. Steve and his wife of forty-five years, Dona, also known as Noah, have three grown children and live in Morris County, New Jersey.

Steve can be contacted at:

Alpha Nurd
Post Office Box 7101
Hackettstown, NJ 07840
USA

info@alphanurd.com

www.AlphaNurd.com

CPSIA information can be obtained
at www.ICGtesting.com
Printed in the USA
JSHW011940200323
39193JS00001B/7